# BOTH FEET IN THE AIR

# BOTH FEET IN THE AIR

*An Airline Pilot's Story*


by

A. S. JACKSON

TERENCE DALTON LIMITED
LAVENHAM . SUFFOLK
1977

Published by
TERENCE DALTON LIMITED
ISBN 0 900963 73 5

*Photoset in 10/12pt English*

Printed in Great Britain at

THE LAVENHAM PRESS LIMITED
LAVENHAM        .        SUFFOLK

# Contents

# Index of Illustrations

# Introduction

WHEN war broke out in Europe in September 1939 I was enjoying my summer holidays from school. A year later the Battle of Britain was being won in the skies above London and the south of England and no one who lived there at that time will forget the sight of those battles or their pride in the young men who flew the Hurricanes and Spitfires.

In September 1940 I was still below the age for call-up but volunteers were being accepted for flying duties in the Royal Air Force whose age limit was lower than that of the army and navy. When I applied to the recruiting office it was necessary to express a preference for selection as pilot, observer or wireless operator cum air gunner. Not at that time qualified to drive a motor car or even a motor cycle I thought that the interviewing board would consider it gross impertinence to offer myself for pilot training so I placed observer before pilot in order of preference. Furthermore I have never been mechanically minded and was convinced that any contact between myself and my aircraft engine in the manner of the legendary Biggles would prove quite disastrous. I had very little idea what the observer's duties comprised but I visualised myself pointing out towns, rivers and features of the landscape and generally making observations.

In due course I appeared before the aircrew candidates' board which was composed of a trio of elderly and most amiable pilots whom any boy would have been pleased to claim as uncles. After a few minutes discussion on my hobbies and the games I claimed to have excelled in at school it became apparent that they had not bothered to look at my listing of preferences because I heard myself being congratulated upon my enrolment for pilot training. Too amazed to question their wisdom I stammered out my thanks and left the room.

It was the war that introduced me into aviation and many of the most senior British airline pilots still flying today owe their present positions to their choice of service over thirty years ago. Some excellent and exciting books have been written by those who served with great gallantry and distinction during the war years. My own R.A.F. service was far too commonplace to be worthy of description. Life in the airlines has been quite different and of absorbing interest to me and with the passing of my fiftieth birthday there is one question which I am asked more and more often.

"What will you do when you retire from flying?"

Sometimes the question is differently phrased. "Will you be offered a manager's post somewhere: Bermuda perhaps or Tokyo or Hong Kong?"

"No," I reply. There would be little incentive for the men who have served for as many years as oneself but on the ground if the plum jobs went to former pilots.

"What will you do?"

Frankly I don't know. I hope to enjoy a few more busy years on the world's air routes. It comes as a bit of a shock to realise how many years have passed since the Second World War ended. Today the sons and daughters of my colleagues are flying alongside us as pilots and stewardesses.

"Will you miss it when you have to give it all up?"

One remembers long duty "days" that started with a pick-up when everyone else was going to bed; delayed departures due to unserviceability or fog; arriving home days later than expected due to rescheduling of services. Missed family birthdays and anniversaries and all the occasions when one has been told: "Please try and be home for . . ."

One remembers all that but all the pleasant memories do stand out; the old friendships, the meetings "down the route" with other crews, drinking after the flying is over in bars, by swimming pools or squashed into a hotel bedroom.

"We will meet in my room in half an hour. Don't be too long. Bring a glass."

We brought a glass or the tooth mug and the flasks of spirits or cans of beer which the Customs officers had permitted us to keep.

"Will you miss it?"

I know that I shall. Will I forget it all? Certainly not. This book is an attempt to recapture some memories of one pilot's working life.

*For Stephanie*

The author with his father and brother in front of a B.O.A.C. Argonaut. Santiago, Chile.

# CHAPTER ONE

# B.O.A.C. in Wartime, L.A.N.-Chile in Peace

I MADE my first application to join a civil airline from a tent in Burma in 1945. The Japanese had just surrendered and I realised that I would be one of many thousands of pilots who had absolutely no other qualification and would wish to use the only skill they knew.

I wrote to British Latin American Airlines who duly sent an application form for completion and return. There was a space for a passport sized photograph to be fixed to the form and for a time I was stumped. How did one obtain such a photograph in the middle of Burma. Then I remember that my R.A.F. "escape kit" contained several of these along with maps, currency and a button which was really a compass. It had been taken at my operational training unit where the Intelligence officer had been in despair because almost every airman had borrowed the one civilian tie and jacket which hung in the photographic unit. The pattern was distinctive and the Intelligence officer was convinced that the Germans would recognise it every time they interrogated one of our pilots who used the photograph on his escaper's documents.

The airline had not at that time commenced operations but they intended to establish routes to South America. Five shipping companies had joined together to form the Company and they appointed Air Vice Marshal D. C. T. Bennett to be Chief Executive. Before long the incoming Labour government of 1945 nationalised the Company and it became British South American Airways Corporation but the original board of directors continued in office.

I had applied to B.S.A.A. because my family had been established in South America for several generations. My great-grandfather had left Wakefield in Yorkshire and founded a nitrate business in Chile. Consequently I have dual British and Chilean nationality.

In 1941 I had joined the R.A.F. and obtained my "wings" before the end of the year. In April 1942 I was posted, provided with a rail warrant and instructed to report to the Grand Spa Hotel in Bristol. On arrival there I found it to be the wartime headquarters of B.O.A.C. There was rather a perfunctory interview with an official who made it clear that the airline was obliged to accept whomsoever the R.A.F. vouchsafed to them and his dismay at the youth and inexperience of about a dozen of us assembled before him was very apparent. In 1942 R.A.F. pilots with less than two hundred flying hours had already been engaged in operations against the enemy. It must have been some small grain of comfort to him that we were to be employed as second officers which was the rank of B.O.A.C.'s most junior pilots. As a result of this posting I obtained eighteen months' experience of civil flying albeit in the very peculiar circumstances of the war years.

The aircraft on which I made my first flight as a B.O.A.C. co-pilot in 1942.     *British Airways*

The flying boat base was in Poole Harbour with maintenance carried out at Hythe near Southampton where the old hangar and slipways can still be seen. The aircraft then in service were an assortment of types. Two Hercules-engined Short boats "Golden Hind" and "Golden Horn"; two Pegasus-powered Short boats "Cathay" and "Champion" and "Clare" with Perseus engines. There were also two Catalinas with a top speed of ninety knots but their two Pratt and Witney engines and ample fuel capacity gave them a greater range than the other four-engined machines. Modern practice frowns upon a pilot flying several types concurrently in case he becomes confused and makes a mistake when handling the controls but in wartime other priorities arise. The Catalinas did not have flaps

"Golden Hind." *British Airways*

but after take-off the floats were retracted flush with the wing and extended again prior to landing.

Captain Bailey who had been with Imperial Airways, the forerunners of B.O.A.C., since 1924 gave each of us a swift conversion on to the various types of aircraft. A few months later the flying career of this kindly man was ended when one of his hands was severed by the propeller of a Catalina. He had been waiting to take off from Poole Harbour and had opened the hatch above his head to wave away a launch which was obstructing the take-off area.

Catalina in flight.



The pilot of a flying boat has to understand the effect of wind and tide when manoeuvring on the water, particularly when approaching the mooring buoy at the conclusion of the flight. It was the radio officer's job to stand in the bow and lift the noose off the buoy on to the bollard protruding from the aircraft. His ability to do this depended in great measure upon the captain's skill in bringing the flying boat alongside the buoy at a slow speed. Furious recriminations sometimes followed a botched approach and I have seen radio officers sometimes dragged into the sea after leaning out too far from the bow of a swiftly moving aircraft.

During the war sailing was prohibited in Poole Harbour but permission was granted to B.O.A.C. for instruction to be given to those like myself who were ignorant of the art of watermanship. The owner of a sailing boat was delighted to be asked to instruct us and under his watchful eye we tacked around the considerable number of naval craft moored in readiness for the invasion of Europe. We learnt the rudiments of sailing but although I was occasionally allowed to land an aircraft I do not recall any captain inviting me to try and moor up.

B.O.A.C.'s flying boat base at Hythe, Hants.                    *British Airways*

In May 1942 Malta was under siege and much of North Africa was in enemy control. The role of our flying boats was to carry passengers of high priority, whether admirals or generals, ship's cooks or nurses, between Britain and West Africa whence they were taken by landplanes to their destination in the war zone. Clearly the aircraft would have to refuel more than once en route to West Africa. The first landing place was Foynes on the river Shannon in Eire. Our departure from Foynes was timed to enable the aircraft to fly under cover of darkness and to be safely over the neutral territory of Portugal by daybreak.

The second stop was Lisbon where we landed on the river Tagus. It was a fascinating city to visit in wartime with lights blazing in contrast to the black-out at home, no shortages of food or goods and the bookshops selling both British and German newspapers. Before we departed southbound the crew called at the British Embassy to obtain a weather forecast from the resident meteorologist. His office window was blacked out but only because his activities in the office had been watched with interest from the Germany Embassy which overlooked it.

The third stop was Bathurst in Gambia. We would always take off from Lisbon at night and extinguish the navigation lights as we left Portugal's territorial limits. This was the longest sector and sometimes took fifteen hours in a Catalina but less on the other types. The crew comprised two pilots, a navigator, a radio officer and a flight engineer. Any sleep had to be taken on the softer items of cargo such as mail bags. The Catalinas seldom carried more than half a dozen passengers among the general cargo. The Short flying boats, once so elegant and spacious, had been stripped of all their interior furnishing to reduce unnecessary weight. A steward was seldom carried so boxed meals were provided for the crew and the twenty or so passengers. There was rather a primitive heating system which few of us could control and after an explosion of steam the ice age set in and we sat huddled in coats and under rugs for the remainder of the flight. The passengers invariably travelled in civilian clothes with passports listing some non-military occupation.

There were several accidents. All on "Clare" perished when an engine caught fire as the aircraft was nearing its destination, Bathurst. A Catalina was destroyed at Poole Harbour when it struck a submerged object during its landing run. "Golden Horn" caught fire over Lisbon and crashed in the Tagus.

This aircraft had been engaged upon a test flight after an engine change and the regular staff at the little flying boat jetty at Cabo Ruivo, a couple of customs officers, coffee shop waitresses and one or two wives of local staff had begged the captain to allow them to go on the flight in place of ballast. Unfortunately for them he had agreed. When the engine caught fire smoke had filled the cockpit and impaired the pilot's forward vision as they attempted to alight on the river. Only two survivors were rescued by a launch.

To replace the lost aircraft Sunderlands were delivered to B.O.A.C. These were the military derivation of the Empire flying boats and an improvement in performance was achieved by their use of variable pitch propellers in place of the simple "fine" or "coarse" selection available on the original aircraft. The forward gun turret of the Sunderland had been removed and replaced by a metal fairing leaving a gap which allowed an icy draught to pass throughout the length of the aircraft.

B.O.A.C. Sunderland on the slipway at Hythe. *Pictorial Press*

A Sunderland touches down. *Pictorial Press*

I flew on all these types and by the time I had completed my eighteen months secondment the landings of allied troops in North Africa had resulted in the final expulsion of the German troops from that continent. My final trip with B.O.A.C. was to deliver the one remaining Catalina to Qantas, the Australian airline, at Lake Koggola in Ceylon. On my return I flew as a passenger by B.O.A.C. flying boat to Cairo then by B.O.A.C. Liberator via Tripoli and Lisbon to Lyneham in Wiltshire. The small trickle of seconded R.A.F. pilots of whom I had been one of the first had expanded greatly. Many of the newcomers had completed two tours of operations with bomber or coastal squadrons and were set fair for a long career in civil flying if they so wished. Yet in appearance B.O.A.C. had become more military and less civil. In the autumn of 1943 when I returned to the R.A.F. the civil markings on most of the B.O.A.C. aircraft were being replaced by R.A.F. roundels and the crews were required to wear R.A.F. uniform. The reason for this was political, some of the Allies expressing concern at the manner in which B.O.A.C. appeared to be establishing itself on so many main routes even before the war was won.

In normal times the flying boat tradition and the mystique that surrounded it had held a great attraction for many pilots. As at sea nautical terms were used exclusively and captains signed documents above the word master. I must confess that I never fell under the spell as I found their slow speed exasperating, the business of mooring an intolerable nuisance and the dependence on launches for passengers, baggage and all the minutiae an added disadvantage. Even so the development and expansion of civil aviation opened horizons for the future which did interest me very much.

* * * * * *

A Sunderland in flight over the Pyramids.                    *British Airways*

On my return to England from Burma early in 1946 I went for an interview with B.S.A.A. I was not yet due to be demobilised but was entitled to a return trip to Chile under the terms of a new Air Ministry order concerning volunteers from neutral countries. The B.S.A.A. headquarters was in Grafton Street in London and I was interviewed by Captain Gordon Store, one of several ex-B.O.A.C. pilots who had been brought in to organise the new airline. Services had just started with Lancastrians, which were converted Lancaster bombers and carried a maximum of thirteen passengers. The first pilots recruited had been hand-picked by Air Vice Marshal Bennett from the Pathfinder Force he had created during the war. Most of them had held the rank of Wing Commander. Their initial task had been to obtain civil pilots' and navigators' licences. I was advised to apply again when I had acquired both these licences myself.

There was an indefinite period to wait for a passage on a boat bound for South America and I spent this time studying for the necessary licences at the School of Navigation attached to the University of Southampton. It was one of the only places then offering a course. At the start I was astonished and dismayed at the very comprehensive range of subjects which I was required to master and realised very early that I would require months rather than weeks to prepare for the examinations. Having overcome this mental hurdle the small band of regular students got a wry enjoyment at the discomfiture of those who came hopefully to the school for only one week's course of study, imagining that they needed to brush up on a few basic subjects forgotten since they had done their pre-flight ground instruction in the R.A.F.

I took the examination in the huge ballroom of a London club which had been rented by the Air Ministry to accommodate the large number of applicants for civil licences. There was then a very long period, perhaps six to eight weeks, to wait before the results were notified, owing to the lack of sufficient examiners to mark the papers. During this period of waiting I faced an unexpected dilemma. The R.A.F. became aware that it would be scarcely worth while sending me to Chile and bringing me back again for demobilization. Therefore they offered me an instant release and a one-way ticket instead. I had been very fortunate to have had the time to study for the licences whilst still drawing my R.A.F. pay but I was faced with the need for a quick decision. I had intended to return from Chile, join B.S.A.A. and marry, in that order. Now I had to change my plans completely and my fiancée and I arranged a hurried marriage by special licence so that she too would qualify for a passage to Chile. We were married the day after I had sat the last of the examinations and were on the high seas bound for Buenos Aires before I had learned the results. If I had failed any subject there would be no opportunity to re-sit it. If I had passed then the licence would probably be recognised by most other countries and I could join an airline in South America.

After a journey of several weeks in the usual cramped conditions of a troopship, officers separated from their wives and sleeping and eating on mess decks, Buenos Aires finally appeared on the skyline. We lined the decks and welcomed our approaching release from that ship. The majority of those on board were volunteers from the Argentine and some had brought back wives from Britain for whom everything would be new and strange. All of us looked forward to a real bed with clean sheets and after years of rationing, many were contemplating with relish the prospect of devouring an enormous beef steak.

These happy images were banished from our minds by the lurch and shudder of the ship as it slewed off course and stuck fast in the mud on the approach into the harbour. For a further three days and nights we waited muttering mutinously whilst the food got worse and the angle of the ship prevented the lavatory system from functioning properly. A flotilla of tugs blew whistles and pulled fruitlessly this way and that. Then I received good news. I had asked my wife's family to open the letter from the examination board and to cable me the results. Their message was brief. "Congratulations. You are airborne."

I had not been to Chile since 1937, nine years earlier, when after a bout of pleurisy I had been temporarily removed from boarding school in England and had returned to my family to enjoy a warm summer and miss the English winter. My fluency in Spanish was therefore considerably less than perfect but L.A.N.-Chile, the national airline to whom I applied for work, were very understanding and helpful. My licences were accepted and I was engaged together with several other ex-R.A.F. pilots who had been born in Chile.

The country is about two thousand miles in length from north to south but narrow with the Pacific ocean on its western shore and the Andes mountains separating it from its eastern neighbour Argentina. L.A.N.'s routes from Santiago, the capital, extended to Arica in the extreme north and to Punta Arenas in the far south. In 1946 the only route outside Chile was to Buenos Aires. Three types of aircraft were in use, the Douglas D.C.3. still familiar as the Dakota, the Lockheed Lodestar which during the war had been developed into the Hudson coastal aircraft and the much smaller and original Lockheed Electra. All of these were of course twin-engined and the pilots were expected to fly all three types. I had flown the Dakota in the R.A.F. and was given a verbal briefing on the other two, sitting in their cockpits with an instructor. Subsequently I operated on all three aircraft as a co-pilot.

L.A.N.-Chile Douglas DC3 aircraft at Los Cerrillos Airport.                    *L.A.N.-Chile*

Lockheed Electra of L.A.N.-Chile.

L.A.N.-Chile

I was very surprised to notice that the compass compensation cards on some of the aircraft were dated anything up to four years earlier, a very long time for compasses to go uncorrected. The reason was startlingly simple. No night flying was done at all. Navigation was almost entirely by visual reference to the ground during the long summer months of fine clear weather and in the winter when the sky was obscured by a layer of cloud the aircraft flew "on top", navigating by reference to easily recognised features at the foothills of the Andes mountains. These had names like the "Saddleback" and "Tiger's stripes". Very few of the airfields had runways but most possessed one radio beacon which enabled pilots to carry out an instrument let-down when necessary.

Some of the aircraft had autopilots but they were seldom put to use as the sectors were fairly short and the pilots preferred to fly manually. All the pilots were born in Chile and most came to the airline from the Chilean air force. Nearly all spoke good English having been transferred for periods of their military service to United States air force units for aircraft type conversions and other duties. My attempts to improve my Spanish were often frustrated by their delight in answering me in English and when I joined a gathering of pilots they often resumed their conversation in English. Though exquisitely polite this did not improve my command of their language. The airline had no domestic competition and therefore needed to pay their staff only a little more than air force pay to obtain the pick of the available applicants. Thus as a new co-pilot I was paid the equivalent of ten pounds sterling weekly which even in 1946 was insufficient to cover all expenses.

Very few pilots could afford to run a car but the airline sent crew buses each morning to collect those rostered to operate services. In the evening we were driven home. The airline were punctilious about notifying one's family in the event of a delayed return. In my six months' service with L.A.N. I did not have any mechanical delays, but I was occasionally held up by weather. I had applied for a telephone to be installed in my flat but as in Britain there was a long waiting list and I waited in vain. When necessary a driver would be sent from the airport with an explanatory note to my wife. L.A.N.-Chile was a small happy airline, keen to obtain more modern equipment. The servicing of the aircraft was excellent.

There were some charming touches to the schedules. There was a circuit to be flown over a large field half-way between Santiago and Concepcion, a town to the south of the capital. When there was a passenger to be picked up the local agent rode about the field on a white horse and we would know that we were required to land. He would give each of the pilots a bottle of the local wine and we would hand out that day's Santiago newspapers. The Chileans are interested in politics and are also avid soccer and horse-racing fans. Iquique in the north of Chile was once a prosperous port and a centre of the almost defunct nitrate trade. My father had been born there. We landed our aircraft on the old abandoned racecourse watched by a few people who sat in the old grandstand.

The most interesting route was across the Andes mountains to Buenos Aires. Only the British with the Lancastrian had an aircraft capable of carrying passengers above all the peaks. Like the other airlines L.A.N. flew at about thirteen thousand feet through the mountain passes. Pressurised cabins were still in the future. The crew had oxygen masks, but the passengers sucked tubes of oxygen for the half hour or so that we remained at a high level. In the morning the Andes passage was often smooth. The return flight from Buenos Aires in the afternoon was much rougher and unpleasant for everyone when the heat rising from the land strengthened the convection currents. The route through the Andes was a series of doglegs. Three radio stations in the mountains reported the cloud conditions and pilots attempting the flight were given up-to-date information to enable them to assess the chances of success. On a cloudless day it was an exhilarating experience to fly through the "cordillera" with Mount Aconcagua towering above one, at over 23,000 feet, and the most timid passenger could not fail to appreciate the beauty of the peaks, mountain lakes and permanent glaciers. One could even see the statue of "the Christ of the Andes" at the point along the pass which marked the border between Chile and Argentina.

Beauty was transformed into menace when the weather broke and every mountain, crag and peak was suddenly wrapped in dark lowering cloud and all of these seemed ever closer to the aircraft. There was no other course but to bank around in a steep turn and fly back on a reverse track. In poorer visibility disaster awaited any pilot who became confused and flew along the wrong valley. The "cordillera" route had been pioneered by the French airman Mermoz flying for Aeropostale, the forerunners of Air France in the nineteen-twenties. The "bolthole" on the Argentine side of the Andes was Mendoza. An excellent hotel there looked after the planeloads of frustrated passengers who were occasionally grounded for days on end. Sometimes they would decide to conclude their journey by train through the Andes to Chile. Whilst they remained in the hotel they were required to settle their own bills. Acts of God such as the weather were not held to be the responsibility of the airlines.

I had rented a flat in the suburb of Santiago known as "El Golf" after a local club. We had an excellent view of the Andes from the sitting room balcony and it was a joy to watch the mountains on a clear evening when they glowed in a rosy hue as sunset approached. But when the skies looked more threatening and the clouds towered over the Andes my wife learnt to anticipate my probable delayed return and the driver with his note from the airport came as no surprise.

My wife and I were delighted with our small flat; we enjoyed Chile's wonderful climate, we made many friends and had time to pay visits to the coastal resorts like Vina del Mar, to ride and to swim. A few of my friends who had joined B.S.A.A. visited us from time to time, envied our apparent good fortune and spoke of the awful winter they were enduring in Britain with no let-up as the spring of 1947 approached. It was with considerable astonishment therefore that they received the news that I had decided to leave Chile and return to England to join B.S.A.A.

The reason was almost entirely financial. I had arrived in Chile with enough money in the bank to furnish a flat and supplement for a limited time the inadequate salary which I was paid. When the money was exhausted I could count upon my final R.A.F. gratuity but that would not keep us for very long. True I was about to be promoted to captain but the increased salary would only delay the approaching financial disaster, not prevent it. I used to wonder how the Chilean pilots subsisted but very few of the younger ones were married and many lived in a large family home which contained several generations. If I was going to leave Chile it would have to be whilst I still had sufficient funds to cover the move.

One morning I was flying a Lodestar to Buenos Aires and I had completed a long spell at the controls whilst the captain was reading his morning newspaper before he finally cast it down and offered to do a little flying himself. I picked up the newspaper and noticed a photograph of Air Vice Marshal Bennett on the front page at the head of a news item.

Apparently he was due to arrive in Buenos Aires early that afternoon on a flight from London. I decided there and then to go and see him and ask for a job with B.S.A.A.

When we landed at Moron airport, the old grass airfield serving Buenos Aires, the traffic staff of B.S.A.A. were in evidence awaiting the arrival of their Lancastrian and they answered my enquiry with the information that Bennett had been booked into the *Plaza Hotel* where he would address a press conference later in the day. Fortunately my crew were not required to fly back to Santiago until the following morning so I had time to write down a few notes about my qualifications and flying experience and to wait as long as was necessary to speak to Bennett at the *Plaza Hotel.* Soon after I arrived there I recognised him as he came into the lobby accompanied by his local manager and when I intercepted him and asked him if he could spare a few minutes on a private matter after the press conference he was pleasantly agreeable. After some time it became apparent that the reporters were leaving the hotel and a little while later I was beginning to wonder whether Bennett had departed by another route when he reappeared. "Good gracious," he remarked, "I had forgotten all about you. What was it?"

"These are my qualifications," I told him, handing over the brief notes I had prepared. "My original application to join B.S.A.A. as a pilot is in London. I would like to apply again."

He read quickly what I had written and asked if I had ever been involved in a crash and also whether my present employer would willingly release me to a competitor. I was able to satisfy him on these points. "Then you call on Taylor, our man in Santiago and tell him that I have engaged you. You are authorised to fly to London as super-numerary crew as soon as you are able to do so. When will that be?"

"In about a month," I answered and began to add that I was married. "You go free," he interrupted. "You will have to pay the fares of your wife and any children."

To have glanced at that newspaper on that day whilst flying to Buenos Aires seemed to me to be an act of providence. I could just afford to pay my wife's fare. Next I had to decide what to do about the flat and the furniture and where we would live in England. On the following day I was flying back to Santiago with my mind much engaged with all the plans to be made. During the flight the captain with whom I had regularly been crewed revealed that he had been chosen to go to the United States to collect the first of the new Martin 202 airliners which L.A.N. had ordered and he offered to arrange things so that I accompanied him. He was astonished at the news of my own plans and I was at pains to explain that I simply could not afford to stay in L.A.N., much as I had enjoyed the many advantages of living in Chile.

I rented my flat furnished to a member of the British Embassy staff in Santiago, thus avoiding the substantial loss which I would have incurred if I had been obliged to sell our new furniture so soon. Fortunately L.A.N. made no difficulties about releasing me. The only jarring note was the perplexity of my friends and relatives in Chile that we should wish to leave and the equal incredulity of my wife's people in England that we should choose to return in the midst of the appalling 1947 winter to endure tighter rationing and controls than had been experienced during the war years.

# CHAPTER TWO

# Air Routes to South America

WITH their first flight departing from London's Heathrow Airport on 1st January, 1946, B.S.A.A. had wasted little time in inaugurating a British air link with South America but competition was soon to come from Air France, Iberia and K.L.M. Royal Dutch Airlines with Alitalia and Scandinavian airlines following. Before the war the Americans and the French had dominated the international air lines to South America and the part played by the French in opening the routes on which we in B.S.A.A. were to follow has been superbly described by the pilot Antoine de St Exupery in his books *Wind, Sand and Stars* and *Night Flight*.

When I joined B.S.A.A. in March 1947 the company was operating three flights a week across the south Atlantic via Lisbon, Dakar and Natal to Rio de Janeiro. One flight continued to Montevideo and Buenos Aires and another made the complete journey to Santiago. This route was flown by a York as far as Buenos Aires whereupon the same crew flew a Lancastrian over the Andes to Santiago. The normal cruising level on either type was ten thousand feet but oxygen masks were fitted on the Lancastrian which had been designed as a high level bomber. The Lancastrian was thereafter flown by another crew via Lima to Barranquilla in Colombia, Jamaica, Nassau (Bermuda), and the Azores to London. One stewardess looked after a maximum of thirteen passengers and the divided skirt of her uniform allowed her to climb modestly backwards and forwards across the main spar with the passengers' trays. The York had twenty-one seats and no gymnastic feats were required. All the aircraft were named with the prefix "Star" and bore names like "Star Dust", "Star Haze"; they were referred to as Starliners and a strange emblem on the nose of each one was supposed to represent a Starman. The stewardesses were called Stargirls. Most of them came directly to the airline from the W.A.A.F. or W.R.N.S. and some of them spoke Spanish or Portuguese having originally been volunteers from South America.

B.S.A.A. was one of the first British airlines to employ stewardesses and there were considerable numbers of applicants for the few vacancies. Their pay was pitifully low, under three pounds a week. One of them related to me an account of her interview prior to her acceptance by the airline. She was told very bluntly that she would always have her own room when on service and a key to lock it. Accordingly the Company did not wish to hear of any complaints by girls of propositions by amorous pilots. Girls came cheaply and were easily replaced. Good licensed pilots were a rare breed and would not be dispensed with for frivolous reasons. "On my first trip," she said, "I locked the door and wedged a chair against the lock but nothing untoward threatened. So next trip I just locked the door. After

B.S.A.A. Stargirls pose before an Avro York.

*British Airways*

my third trip my morale was really shattered. I gave up locking the door and took to looking up and down the passage and wondering what everyone else was doing.''

Although the Company had a board of directors under a chairman chosen by the shipping companies the strong personality of Air Vice Marshal Bennett, so well known to the public from the publicity accorded to the activities of his Pathfinder Force, ensured that B.S.A.A. was generally thought of as ''Bennett's airline''. Before the war he had himself been an Imperial Airways captain and his aim was to make B.S.A.A. into a highly efficient airline with each individual offering willing and loyal service and what would today be called a high productivity. To him B.O.A.C., the senior corporation, was at that time grossly overmanned and an example of which to beware. An intensely patriotic man he intended operating only British aircraft with British equipment. The delivery of the Tudor IV, our first pressurised aircraft, was eagerly awaited and future planning envisaged the use of Princess flying boats and the De Havilland Comet I.

Three former Imperial Airways captains had been engaged to form a nucleus for the new airline and one of these was appointed operations manager. The remaining pilots were almost all from the R.A.F. or Dominion air forces. There were two Canadians who had been demobilised in England and had for a short while run their own air service with a single-engined aircraft. They had observed that the railways in Britain adequately served those travelling north and south but that journeys across the breadth of the country were made lengthy and tedious by the necessity for frequent changes. They had hoped to tap this market but almost their only passengers were bookmakers requiring transport to various racecourses. The bookmakers were lavish with tips both financial and equine but the enterprise had been a failure. There were also three Australians who had flown three Airspeed Oxfords all the way to England for a fee of fifty pounds. They had even had difficulty collecting that modest sum until the largest of them tracked down the business man who was supposed to pay them to the lounge of the Royal Aero Club. There he shattered the peace of that august establishment by shouting "I want my money" in stentorian antipodean tones. Needless to say he got it without further delay.

Those selected as station managers at the airports overseas were also former R.A.F. pilots and two of them had been air attachés. The headquarters staff in Grafton Street was very small and one came to know everybody else in a very short space of time. My first impression was of belonging once more to a really good keen squadron. In the next two years the Company was to be rocked by disaster after disaster but even at the end, after Bennett had gone and an amalgamation with B.O.A.C. was upon us, the old loyalty was still there when the great majority of the employees gathered at Caxton Hall to protest at the loss of the airline's identity.

My instructions were to report to Hut 43 on the north side of London Airport on the 10th March, 1947. Those huts were still there over a quarter of a century later but then

This hut was B.S.A.A.'s Operations Headquarters at London Airport in 1947. *Don Brown*

Marquee for passenger handling. Heathrow, 1947.

*British Airways*

there were also caravans, marquees and former military trailers serving as offices and passenger reception rooms. I reported in Hut 43 to Captain Alabaster who was trying to keep warm at a desk by a coke stove. He explained that I would be required to obtain a navigator's licence, first class, within a few months and he gave me some notes on the York and Lancastrian aircraft, neither of which I had flown before, so that I could take the written examination on these two types and thereby obtain the necessary endorsement on my pilot's licence. I was introduced to other pilots in Hut 43, many of them wearing their R.A.F. greatcoats with leather buttons in place of the original brass ones, with trousers tucked into flying boots because of the intense cold. "It's good to be in civvies again," one of them remarked.

In addition to the written examination I had also to make six take-offs and landings on both the York and Lancastrian to obtain the licence endorsement but the regulations then in force allowed airlines to send out aircraft with only the captain licensed on type and possessing a navigation licence whilst the first officer might have his pilot's licence endorsed

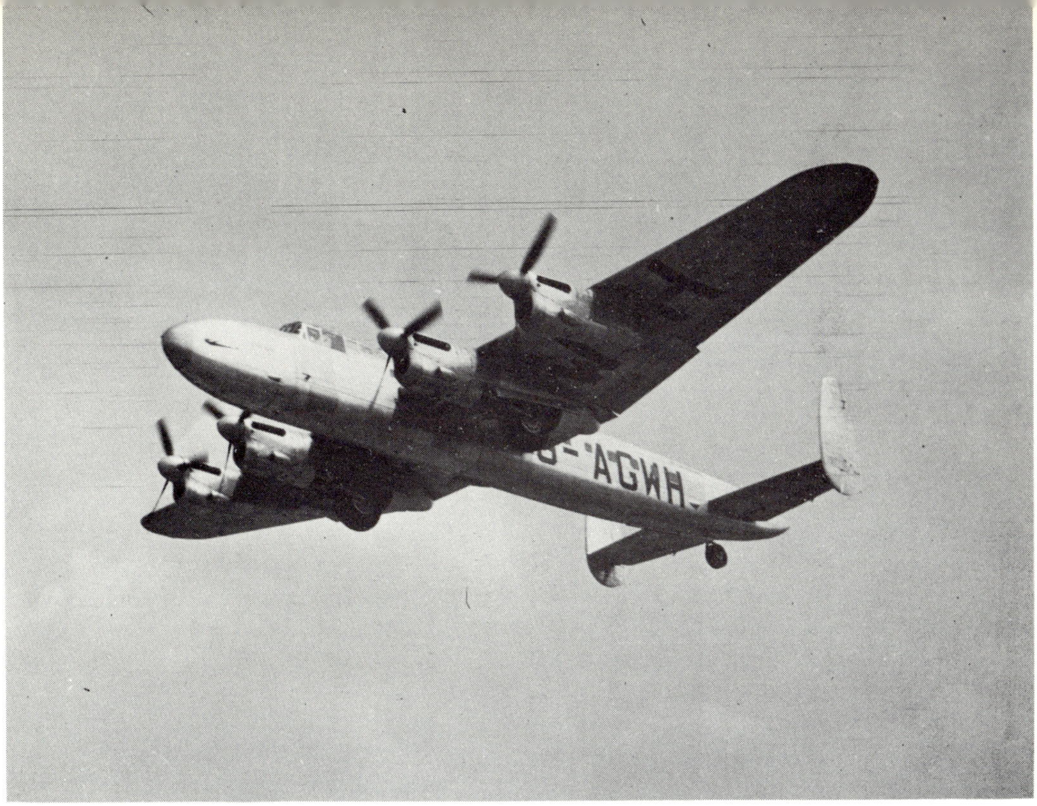

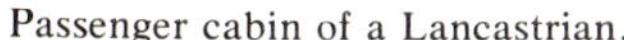

Avro Lancastrian in flight. *British Airways*

Passenger cabin of a Lancastrian. *Don Brown*

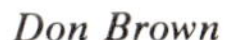

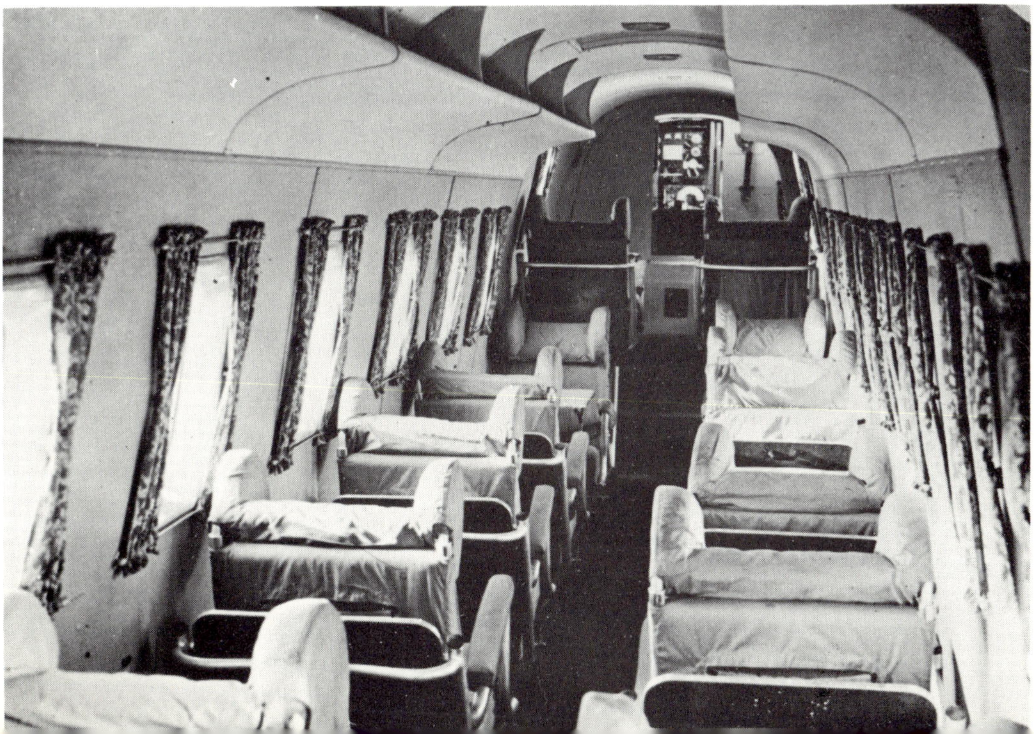

on a Liberator or even a light aircraft and the second officer might be navigating a sector without a navigation licence of any kind. The reason for this was the need to get services going around the world as soon as possible. It placed an enormous responsibility on the Captain who invariably navigated the oceanic sector himself. He was certainly worth every penny of the one thousand pounds a year which he was paid. The licensing authorities were not at all happy with the situation but under pressure from the airlines continually postponed the stiffer rules and regulations which they knew to be necessary.

Having taken the type rating examinations I was most dismayed a short while later to learn that I had failed on both aircraft and hurried anxiously to the office of the Air Registration Board to discover where I had gone wrong. Fortunately the official whom I saw did not resent the enquiry and produced my work. Apparently the drawing of the fuel system which I had faithfully memorised and reproduced had been "simplified" in the notes I had studied to the exclusion of a number of non-return valves and this was too much for the examiner. Resentfully I paid the entrance fee again and re-sat the papers. I also complained in Hut 43 about the inadequacy of their drawings in the issued notes. "Ah yes! the non-return valves. I thought we had warned everybody about those. Bad luck," they said.

Even before I had made my first flight with B.S.A.A. I had the incredible good fortune to find a self-contained flat at a very low controlled rate on the bus route to the airport from Uxbridge. Whilst I might just have afforded to run a car I did not have the capital to buy one and in 1947 ten and fifteen year old models which would today be termed "bangers" were changing hands for several hundred pounds. Accordingly I travelled to the airport on the single decker bus and often fell foul of the conductor who protested that there was no room for my suitcase.

There were never too many pilots in B.S.A.A. and I was soon despatched on a service to Santiago as second officer. Some new pilots and stewardesses also were performing their duties without a uniform because the freezing weather had forced the official outfitters to discontinue work in their unheated premises. Our Stargirl had only a Red Cross badge in her lapel to hint at her occupation.

Every pilot has his own list of places where he is glad of a day off and other places where a "slip" is less than enjoyable. We dearly prized a stay in Lisbon but we normally made only a refuelling stop there and continued the flight to Dakar in West Africa where there was a change of crew. Dakar was about sixteen hours flying time from London, a wearisome stretch in the noisy York even when starting out from Heathrow at the sensible time of ten o'clock in the morning. The accommodation in Dakar, where two pilots and the radio officer shared a room reeking from a mis-used bidet, was squalid indeed, some of the other guests dossing down in the hotel corridors. There was never any hot water and only sea bathing from some good beaches to compensate. Meat was as scarce as in England and the quality of the food very poor. Eagerly we awaited the arrival of the next aircraft from London and prayed that it would land without snags to delay us as the flight to Natal took ten hours and the remaining sector to Rio de Janeiro a further six hours. My friendship with one particular pilot soured almost into hatred as on trip after trip he and I invariably handed over to each other a York with either a severe magneto drop or oil running from

Avro York "Star Leader" of B.S.A.A.



*British Airways*

beneath the engine cowlings or hydraulic fluid pouring from the undercarriage, sometimes all these defects together.

In B.S.A.A. pilots were required to become qualified and proficient navigators and only two non-pilot navigators had been engaged to assist the rest of us in their art. Most of us became keen enthusiasts and always endeavoured to pass within sight of St Paul's rocks, a tiny group, directly on our track between Dakar and Natal. When one failed to see them on clear days the suspicion existed that they must sometimes be below the ocean but, when successful, the delighted navigator would hurry back into the passenger cabin to rouse each weary traveller and insist that they appreciate the privilege of seeing the rocks and the skill that had made the sighting possible. Accurate navigation across the south Atlantic in daylight presented problems. The radio officer could sometimes contact shipping in the area and having established each ship's known position at a certain time, together with its course and speed, obtain bearings from it. The accuracy of fixes obtained in this way depended on the ship's knowledge of its true position and we would often plot such a large "cocked hat" on our charts that we became disinclined to rely too much upon this method. It never failed to astonish me how very slowly most ships proceeded across the ocean. Often they reported their speed as being only four or five knots.

Spitfire accompanies a B.S.A.A. York across the South Atlantic. *D. M. Walbourn*

If we were on schedule both east and westbound crossings were made during the night when astro navigation was possible. However, I remember an occasion when a westbound York operating in daylight was able to give invaluable assistance to another aircraft en route at the same time. This was a Spitfire carrying long range fuel tanks which a demobilised R.A.F. pilot was flying to Argentina whence he had volunteered his services some years before. His fuel reserve was pitifully small but he was able to keep in sight of the York all the way to Brazil. The Spitfire was a photographic reconnaissance version and the pilot hoped to sell it to the Argentine Air Force at the end of his journey.

Natal, unbearably humid and always too hot, was normally only a transit stop. It possessed a large airfield which had been used by the Americans during the war to ferry aircraft across to Bathurst in British Gambia and thence to the Middle East. For a time only a jeep, raised on a plinth and bearing the legend that in it President Roosevelt had toured the airfield, remained to remind anyone interested that Natal had been an important staging post during the war. Later the legend disappeared and not long after that the jeep also. Natal will mainly be remembered by those of us who flew there for the regulation that aircraft arriving from Africa were required to keep all doors and windows closed for about seven minutes whilst an official who had boarded the aircraft sprayed the interior liberally with an insect-killing agent. His principal concern however was to solicit duty-free cigarettes for himself before he could be persuaded to free the sweltering passengers and crew. The premature opening of a door or window cost the company a fifty pound fine.

When finally released everyone on board had to pass through the health department to have a thermometer popped into their mouth. Yellow fever had originally been brought to Brazil by the first aircraft capable of the South Atlantic crossing. Finally we swilled enormous quantities of iced fresh orange juice to revive ourselves and many suffered the inevitable penalty for over-indulgence.

Natal was one of several stations where the wives of station staff voluntarily served as receptionists, often assisting passengers when an aircraft was in transit in the middle of the night. Loyalty and enthusiasm took various forms. I was present when a senior executive from London remarked to an overseas station manager that the uniform of one of the local staff did not conform to the regulation pattern. "Oh, he had that made and paid for it himself," he was told. "His job does not qualify him for a uniform at all."

In the early days of B.S.A.A. the Company's airport manager at Natal submitted an amusing article on life at that station to the airline's own magazine. He wrote about the vagaries of the electrical voltage which ruined any radio or razor or other domestic equipment one might have and he dwelt on the frequent absence of water in the taps despite the torrents of rain that fell in the area. As anyone with knowledge of South Americans will know, perhaps from an interest in football, they possess an extremely volatile and partisan temperament. This article was translated and appeared in a local newspaper under the heading "What one of our guests thinks of us". When the next Company aircraft was in transit at Natal the manager was opening his mail when he heard a disturbance and his investigation revealed an excited crowd letting the air from the tyres of his car. When he ran to intervene he was still unwittingly carrying the knife which he had used to open his mail. His intention was misunderstood and in the resulting fracas he was severely injured. To avoid even further trouble he was put on the aircraft and travelled to Rio de Janeiro for hospital treatment. Later he was recalled from Brazil to avoid further repercussions.

There was always an excellent relationship between passengers and crews. The passengers remained for long periods with the same crew and realised how hard they were worked. The South American passengers clearly thought that the pilots and crew were very young, but during the war what few international air services there were had been conducted by veterans. When they realised that we were not going to throw the aircraft into steep turns as if it was a Spitfire they were quite happy. For our part we noticed that South American passengers had one idiosyncracy which we found nowhere else. The aircraft had barely completed its landing run before they all got up and gathering their possessions made for the exits. All appeals to remain seated and excellent reasons for so doing always fell on deaf ears.

If we were operating behind schedule a night landing would have to be made at the international airport in Rio de Janeiro Bay and some captains were reluctant to risk this as the airport was surrounded by mountain peaks often shrouded in rain and storm clouds. There was the added problem of air traffic from Santos Dumont airport a short distance away in the bay. Therefore there were occasions when we remained at Natal and left before dawn for Rio and made only a transit stop there. Usually we were able to arrive before darkness fell and all of us looked forward to the scheduled night stop in Brazil's capital city. If the weather was fine we obtained permission for a visual descent or flew into the bay through the entrance by the Sugar Loaf mountain with the huge statue of Christ high above the whole harbour and visible for miles around. When it was very cloudy we had to carry out an instrument letdown and unfortunately the B.S.A.A. letdown pattern was held in great disfavour by the Brazilian authorities. Every other airline had the American radio compass whose pointer enabled the pilot to fly directly towards the airfield radio beacon on the required heading and carry out a gradual descent in a fairly tight racetrack pattern until the aircraft broke cloud.

Our aircraft were equipped with the old R.A.F. "twitcher" twin needles for homing on a beacon and great care had to be taken to check whether one in fact had not already flown past it. The safest and most accurate way to use our system for an instrument descent was to fly a "box" pattern with the radio beacon in the centre of the box. This meant that we flew over a much wider area than aircraft in the racetrack pattern. With two different letdowns already in use for two closely situated airports in the harbour the Brazilian authorities served notice on B.S.A.A. that by a certain date we would have to comply with their own published procedures. The airline's reply was that when British radio compasses were available they would be fitted and the quarrel rumbled on with the Brazilians reluctantly postponing the "final " date several times.

After a sixteen hour flight from Dakar the crews looked forward to the comfort of the Serrador Hotel in Rio and forced themselves to stay awake long enough to enjoy dinner in the elegant night club with its two bands and a superb cabaret. We would have welcomed the chance to swim on Copacabana beach but usually we left early the following morning on the next stage of our journey.

The airfields of Brazil were all under military control and a curious system of so-called "route inspection" was practised by the Brazilian Air Force. An officer had to be provided with a free seat on any sector within the country upon demand. Occasionally all the seats were occupied by fare paying passengers and if the military insisted we had to off-load one of them. When this happened we tried to choose a Brazilian subject but the whole system was ridiculous and we had little doubt that the military authorities thought it up as a cheap and convenient way to facilitate their leave and postings arrangements. After a time the transit stop at Natal was altered to Recife and there the Customs Officers insisted on being collected by car from their homes by the airlines themselves. This practice did not cease until all the international airlines got together and agreed that none of them would provide transport for the officials, regardless of the initial delays and appalling inconvenience caused to passengers and schedules.

Our sales manager, newly arrived in Brazil, was aghast at the open flouting of regulations regarding the fares laid down by the International Air Transport Authority and the necessity for paying customs officials to smooth the passage of passengers and goods. Our man in Rio was then Bill Shepherd, a Canadian, and he made certain proposals to our head office which would lessen the unfair competition which we were enduring whilst not being strictly according to the I.A.T.A. rules. He was most indignant when he received a reply that "a British airline must play a straight bat".

"Whoever heard of a straight bat in South America?" he fumed when he told me this story. The local travel agents favoured airlines which paid them commissions substantially above the legal percentage and Shepherd's secretary whom he sent anonymously to one of our competitors returned to report that a huge discount was offered.

A similar situation over fares existed in Argentina whose national airline never published accounts and was used for prestige purposes by the dictator Juan Peron. Buenos Aires, the capital, was reached after a transit stop at Montevideo in Uruguay and the flight along the River Plate lasted one hour. The superstructure of the scuttled German cruiser *Graf Spee* was then still visible off the Uruguayan coast and passengers were invariably interested in the opportunity to see it. Meanwhile the captain was frantically signing a mass of documents required by the Argentine authorities, even to having to countersign the passengers' personal baggage declaration forms.

After the war years the shops, particularly in Buenos Aires, seemed a veritable Mecca to the crews and the luscious steaks served in the restaurants were often too big to be totally consumed. We always asked for a jug of cold milk so severely rationed at home and the waiters became as accustomed to this quaint habit as they were to serving iced water to Americans. After a very comfortable night at the *City Hotel* we continued our journey to Santiago.

Avro York "Star Glitter" at Montevideo's Carrasco airport, Uruguay.                    *D. M. Walbourn*

How odd it seemed to climb so very high, twenty-six thousand feet, for the short crossing of the Andes. How diminished the peaks looked from that level, how boring to circle down above Los Cerillos airport for so very long to avoid discomfort to everyone's ears, before we made our final approach and landing. Now I was back among my friends in Chile.

"Are you still glad you left here?"

"Yes, I'm earning rather more and my rent is a lot less."

"It's so awfully cold in England and there's so little food and petrol rationing."

"I can take food home each trip and anyway I can't afford a car yet."

"Even so it's so damned cold there. It rains all summer too."

The crew had a five day "slip" before the return flight to Buenos Aires on the Lancastrian which arrived in Santiago from Lima at the completion of its mid-Atlantic and west coast service. I have already mentioned that rationing was still very stringent in England and crew members invariably bought food parcels to take home. The usual purchases were canned hams, cream, sausages, eggs and sweets for the children. It was seldom practical to take home fruit other than the canned variety because it became overripe in the final "slip" in Dakar. As well as food and drink, clothing, handbags, nylon stockings, even carpets and rugs were bought as all of these were in very short supply at home.

A Lancastrian is prepared for flight. *British Airways*

On my first trip the radio officer was a former Merchant Navy man, about forty years of age, unlike the majority who were young ex-R.A.F. wireless operators and had become accustomed to being addressed by their fellow crew men as "Wop". Unthinkingly I had been using this expression to our radio officer during the flight and I had attributed his baleful countenance and dour manner towards me to a naturally morose nature. Finally he took me aside and complained that to him "Wop" was an offensive term. Apparently in the Merchant Navy it had taken many years for the wireless operators to be accepted as officers by the captains, mates and deck officers and the battle being finally won they remained touchy on the point.

One of the former marine radio officers was a very jolly man who, revisiting Montevideo for the first time in some years, paid a sentimental journey to the house of a former old friend, the Madame of an establishment, but at a time for a respectable cup of morning coffee. Delighted, she invited him to return that very night and in his honour to have someone, anyone of his choice, on the house. "They are very pro-British there", he maintained, rather modestly.

Standards varied among the radio officers. Not every ex-R.A.F. man who passed the written examinations to become a licensed radio officer turned out to be very competent at obtaining for us weather forecasts, air traffic clearances or any replies to the position reports and other messages, which he was required to transmit. In the R.A.F. many of them had had to be more proficient at air gunnery than in wireless. Our aircraft were equipped with the standard 1939 R.A.F. transmitters and receivers whilst the South American and other radio stations used modern equipment and tapped out morse at very high speeds. In time everyone became more proficient but I remember a flight when the captain was in utter despair at the performance of the radio officer. In those days it was also his duty to raise the civil air ensign and the flag of the host country as we taxied out for take-off or on to the ramp after landing.

"At least you can hoist the correct flags", the captain snarled "and for God's sake remember to bring them in before take off."

Unfortunately, as we took off from Montevideo for Buenos Aires one flag standard was forgotten and was carried away in the airstream.

"Flags!" the captain barked as we turned off the runway in Buenos Aires. The poor radio officer found the Argentine flag and searched frantically for the means to hoist it. Then he realised what he had done, seized the short length of metal which was used to lock the elevators on overnight stops, rigged the flag and held it aloft with his arm. As we left the flight deck the captain summed up the situation but found no words to express his feelings. The radio officer continued to hold up the flag until all had left the aircraft and then he followed us dejectedly into the airport building.

Normally the crew which had travelled to Santiago via the east coast of South America returned by the same route and so did the crew which had arrived through Colombia and Peru. On one occasion a decision was taken to turn round a Lancastrian at Santiago because it was so late and send it north with the crew which had arrived days earlier from Buenos Aires. Signals were accordingly despatched to this effect and I was on the crew which flew to Lima. Unfortunately it was a Sunday and none of our staff in Lima had been advised of our intentions because the cable sent to them had not been delivered. Some members of the company were enjoying a game of cricket at the English Club when they were amazed to see the Lancastrian pass overhead. The teams and spectators must have been even more astonished to see several fielders hastily abandoning the pitch without even waiting for the end of the over. Our original manager at Lima had already left B.S.A.A. to take up a more lucrative position flying for a Peruvian airline. He had heard our aircraft reporting its E.T.A. to the airport and having landed a little earlier himself had been surprised to see none of our staff on duty. So loyally he offered his services and in due course our passengers were even more bewildered to observe the late arriving cricketers in their white flannels assisting with the formalities.

Commanding the first airliner to land at Peru's new Limatambo airport, Captain Derek Walbourn is greeted by the Minister for Air.                                   *D. M. Walbourn*

# CHAPTER THREE

# A Chapter of Accidents

IT HAS never been practicable for an airline to keep the same crew flying together and therefore training procedures have always been designed so that absolutely standard drills are performed by crew members and idiosyncracies in operating eliminated. In this way it is hoped that unacquainted individuals flying together for the first time will perform the necessary actions in exactly the same manner. Nevertheless it is impossible to iron out every quirk and one soon learned the odd ways of different captains. When I was rostered to fly with a senior management pilot I was warned to have available in my brief case some copper wire and a pair of pliers. Thinking this might be a leg-pull I asked another pilot and he replied, "Don't forget to take a pair of pliers and some copper wire. Oh! and don't wear non-regulation socks." Sure enough the captain asked me whether I carried these items and then proceeded to make little hooks and hang cards bearing the compass heading, altitude and other information about the instrument panel before us.

Another captain insisted on his crew wearing their caps in the cramped confines of the cockpit with the radio earphones worn overall, which was extremely uncomfortable. I had only seen this done before in rather bad American films about flying. He abhorred the use of Christian names on the flight deck. There was one who became apoplectic if he saw litter, even a sweet paper, on the cabin floor and yet another with a sensitive nose who passed round Amplex tablets to his crew. Some captains like one to "trim" the propellers as one taxied to a halt after a flight. This meant stabbing the starter buttons after each engine had stopped until all four of them carried one propeller blade absolutely vertical. "I hate to see propeller blades just anywhere," I was once chided. "All it needs is the midwife's touch." I think that this idea had originated on flying boats. It was a dangerous practice on landplanes since as each aircraft came to a halt it was invariably approached by numerous loaders, cleaners and mechanics. They did not take kindly to near-misses from sharply kicking propellers which had been stationary moments before.

With only three services a week to South America's eastern coast and one a week from the west coast the crews were away as long as three weeks at a time because of the "slips" en route and the wait for the next aircraft. The time at home between trips, known as "stand-off" was about a week but this was frequently occupied in the very unpopular pastime of "duty crew". This crew was required to attend the airport daily and carry out any test flights of aircraft that emerged from the hangars after various maintenance checks and also to carry out compass swings when an engine had been changed or anything done which might affect the aircraft's compasses. Regularly it happened that the aircraft were only ready for a test flight when one had spent an entire day idle at the airport and sometimes it became necessary to carry out the "swing" at night. On such occasions two torches were attached to the undercarriage and the luckless crew member assigned to the tripod and astrocompass tramped round the middle of London's cold and windy airport until the aircraft's compasses had been compensated on every necessary heading. I was engaged upon an air test late one summer's evening when I looked down and observed that we were flying above Chesham where my wife's parents lived. I remarked upon this fact to our disgruntled captain. "You have my permission to chuck out the Elsan if you wish," he replied.

The captain of the duty crew was often a senior first officer who was next in line for command. If he felt that he had incurred this task more often than his colleagues he would be less likely to complain. On the first occasion I found myself duty crew captain I waited all day for a York to become ready for an air test. I was very worried by the delay because I had never landed a York at night. The six landings required to be performed for the endorsement of one's licence were invariably carried out by day and in those early days captains were usually reluctant to offer landings at night to first officers whom they scarcely knew. Finally at dusk the aircraft was ready and in the winter gloom visibility was reducing minute by minute. Once airborne there was only the S.B.A., the standard beam approach to help one find the runway. When tuned in this allowed the pilot to hear dots on one side of the correct approach path and dashes on the other, an even note indicating that he was flying on the centre line. Near the runway the centre line was so narrow that he was likely to hear clear dots or dashes and it was difficult to suppress the inclination to make too large an alteration of course to regain the steady note and find the runway.

Before taking off I checked the cloud base, visibility and the expected trend with the tower controller and evidently he appreciated my anxiety about being able to find my way back. When I had finished the test flight and rejoined the circuit I observed white Very lights being fired into the air at the threshold of the runway as I descended towards it. There was then no approach lighting.

There were compensations also for senior first officers. They were sent out in command of the Lancastrian freighter carrying engines or spare parts and stores to stations down the route. In 1947 B.S.A.A. were asked to undertake deliveries of Lincoln bombers purchased by the Argentine air force and I flew one of these to Buenos Aires whilst still ranking as a first officer.

B.S.A.A. had suffered its first serious accident before I had joined when a heavily laden York departing from Bathurst in the Gambia had crashed shortly after take-off with the loss of all on board. The effect of temperature and air density on aircraft performance was not properly compensated for in those days, but the maximum permitted take-off weight of a York was thereafter reduced by two thousand pounds. Operations were moved from Bathurst to Dakar ninety miles to the north which suffered only four months rainfall in the year from the intertropical zone as against eight months rain in Bathurst.

Even so it was at Dakar that the next accident occurred. At about midnight a York was approaching from the north after the long flight from England via Lisbon. The weather forecast for Dakar was good and the captain had been able to talk on his radio to a colleague on the northbound flight which had taken off from Dakar an hour or so earlier.

"There were some patches of mist developing," he was told "but it was not at all bad when we got off."

At Dakar the visibility was falling rapidly when he joined the circuit preparatory landing. The airfield was bereft of any aids to assist a pilot to conduct an instrument approach. The brightest light by far was a lighthouse on the coast which on clear nights was often visible to us a hundred miles away. There was no airfield radio beacon, no approach lighting, just the feeble runway lights.

If the pilot had decided at once to divert to Bathurst he would have landed safely but that is stated with the advantage of hindsight. After he had made several unsuccessful approaches his reserve fuel for a diversion was gone. Finally, committed to make as good a landing as he could the aircraft overshot the runway and was very severely damaged as it came down in an orchard of small trees.

The weather was a subject that worried the pilot to a far greater extent than it does today. The aircraft were poorly equipped to fight ice on the propellers or wings. Another ten years were to elapse before storm warning radar became available on new aircraft. Some airfields were even worse equipped than they had been during the war because the military had left, handing them back to be operated by the country's own administration but taking with them the expensive equipment that they had found it essential to install. Dakar was at that time managed poorly by the French authorities. The refuelling unit once allowed so much water to contaminate the fuel that all the engines of one of our aircraft stopped as it taxied out to the runway. On another occasion the same ground crew topped up the domestic water system of another company's aircraft with glycol and the aircraft had to be recalled after it had begun its flight. After incidents such as these our crews invariably carried out sample checks on fuel uplifts. It followed that the airports of large cities would be better equipped than most, but in 1947 the runway lights of London Airport were a lot less bright than the street lights of the Bath road which runs parallel to one of the main runways.

Without today's weather radar the pilots picked their way as best they could through the fronts that always lay somewhere in the South Atlantic and we also encountered some fearsome storms over Brazil. Should one fly towards the brightest area of the mass of clouds ahead? Some said no; they were bright because those were the clouds towering highest into the sunshine high above the general mass of the clouds: but if one flew into the blackest cloud hoping to avoid the worst convection currents it seemed as if the aircraft was caught in solid water and the hailstones thudding into the windscreen and against the engine cowlings were as worrying as the vicious turbulence. Captain Fieldson suffered the destruction of his windscreen and the failure of an engine in one such storm and made a safe landing at Porto Alegre. At least the York had windscreen wipers although these were only used on the ground or when an aircraft was landing or on take off. The Lancastrian was not so fitted and when circling an airport in rain and also in conditions of poor visibility the pilot might slide back his side window and peer out.

The aircraft that crashed at Dakar was flown by a pilot on his first trip in command of a B.S.A.A. passenger service and another pilot on his first command was flying the Lancastrian "Star Dust" from Buenos Aires to Santiago some weeks later. There was solid cloud piled up over the Andes mountains that day and all the local carriers who used the pass in visual flight conditions had cancelled their trans-Andean services. The mountain Aconcagua is over twenty-three thousand feet high but our aircraft regularly crossed the Andes several thousand feet higher than that. The Lancastrian was in contact with ground radio stations as it approached the mountains and it is probable that the crew flew south for a time to find some break in the clouds and thus avoid a rough crossing. Requests by ground stations for a position report several times brought the answer "Stand by". Later calls went unanswered and after some hours it was apparent that there had been another tragedy.

The air forces of Chile and the Argentine searched the enormous length of the Andes on their frontier for several days without finding any wreckage and abandoned any hope of finding survivors. I arrived in Buenos Aires on a York service at this time and A.V.M. Bennett who had flown from London with us decided to continue the search using a Lancastrian freighter which was then in the area. I accompanied him on a search which lasted several days. In the event that wreckage and survivors were observed we carried parcels wrapped in red cloth to show up against the snow when ejected and Bennett had brought a parachute and skis. The weather on the Argentine side had remained bad and there were time when those of us on board who were flying or merely staring out from the windows grew anxious for our own safety. The clouds at times pressed all about us and the mountains appeared perilously close as we flew up narrowing valleys and then banked steeply round, flying back before we completely lost our bearings. It was a hopeless task. In succeeding years there have been rumours of mountain bandits and smugglers who have found the site of the crash but its position has never been officially established. The threat of the Andes weather was thereafter taken to heart and for a long time crossings were abandoned unless the flight could made in clear skies above cloud. A captain and radio officer were sent to Santiago to take overall command on the mountain sector and the dramatic words "Mountain attack" signalled before each crossing.

There were no legal limits to the length of time a crew could be ordered to remain on duty. An airline made its scheduling arrangements and recognising that there would often be mechanical or other delays during the course of any flight authorised the captain to interrupt the service to avoid "crew fatigue". Some, particularly new captains or very zealous pilots were reluctant to do this and prodigious lengths of duty were sometimes performed. Other captains would ignore the protests of passengers and call a halt for a rest of eight hours or so before proceeding. Sometimes the local staff would question such a decision particularly when they knew that few hotel rooms were available locally or that the quality of the accommodation was very poor and at some considerable distance from the airport. On the other hand it was considered most unreasonable to bring a delayed flight into

London Airport in the middle of the night when passengers would be severely inconvenienced by the lack of onward transport or means of going to their homes. Regularly a stop was made at Lisbon and the flight continued after breakfast in the morning. No such courtesy can be afforded by cost-conscious airlines today with the vastly increased passenger numbers on most flights.

A passenger could hope to travel from London to Santiago in the course of four days in 1947 but he might spend as many days at some point en route if the aircraft became unserviceable and needed an engine change or a new cylinder block and a spare was not held at that place. The next flight might pass through with some empty seats and an argument develop as to who should occupy the available space but for the most part the passengers accepted the hazards. The long sectors were so boring that they were glad to go into the galley and help the Stargirl wash up the crockery in preparation for the next meal and I remember a Company notice being published that strongly discouraged this practice. The meals were not very luxurious and one passenger complained to me that it was "the sort of fare one might expect to be offered if one arrived unheralded at a hotel in Derby on a Sunday".

Whatever aircraft an airline operates there is always a new type being produced which will in due course come into service and in 1947 we in B.S.A.A. awaited the Tudor, one of the first pressurised aircraft to be built in Britain. It had also been ordered in a smaller version by B.O.A.C. who, after demanding an interminable series of modifications, carried out tropical air tests on a Tudor at Khartoum and refused to accept it. Air Vice Marshal Bennett flew the B.S.A.A. Tudor IV, a longer bodied version, to the Caribbean, declared it to be ten per cent better than a Constellation and accepted it.

Air Vice Marshal and Mrs Bennett about to depart on the proving flight of the Avro Tudor. The operating crew (left to right) Radio Officer Chandler, Captain Alabaster, Captain Rodley, First Officer Kerrigan, Second Radio Officer. *Don Brown*

Avro Tudor in flight.

*British Airways*

Pilots are usually eager to transfer to a more modern aeroplane and we looked forward to delivieries from A. V. Roe the manufacturers. A curious rumour circulated among the Stargirls at this time. Speaking to a gathering the Company Medical Officer was surprised to be asked by one of them if continual flying in a pressurised aircraft could render a girl sterile. Considerably taken aback he was not at a loss for an answer. "I should most certainly not count on it if I were you," he replied.

**Whilst still flying Lancastrians and Yorks we had occasional opportunities to do some practice flying on the Tudor IV and also the Tudor I, the type rejected by B.O.A.C. and thereafter made available to us for training purposes.** The position of the undercarriage and flap selectors were reversed in the two versions, a fact which required the pilot to be on his guard. There was a pressurisation panel operated by the officer occupying the navigator's seat and the heating system was also in his control. The pressurisation panel required considerable skill to avoid ear-poppings and general discomfort and the heating system was so inefficient that aircraft sometimes descended of necessity to avoid freezing all on board. I remember a red light which illuminated to warn us against any further attempt to re-start the system. The fuel system was operated by the pilots but there was one cock controlling it below one of the passenger seats. Apart from these disadvantages the Tudor **certainly flew higher than the Yorks and faster than either the York or Lancastrian. It appeared to present no particular handling problems in the air but the huge tail area above the tail wheel made it awkward to taxi, particularly in strong or gusty winds.**

Ill-fortune in the shape of accidents continued to affect our operations. One captain was particularly unlucky. Leaving Bermuda eastbound on a Lancastrian with a full load of fuel he was obliged to shut down an engine and turned back for a landing on the island. Being well above the approved landing weight he carried out the drill for dumping fuel but unfortunately the jettison system was defective, the fuel in one wing failed to flow out to atmosphere and strong fumes penetrated the cockpit. Nauseated by the smell of petrol, and with the aircraft in an asymetric attitude, the pilot finally lined up for his landing approach but selected full flaps too early and had to increase power continuously on his three sound engines as the aircraft descended. This aggravated the asymmetry and made the aircraft more difficult to keep straight by rudder control. The aircraft descended too low on the approach to the runway, the undercarriage wheels striking the seawall and breaking away whilst the aircraft then slithered along the runway on its belly. Luckily all on board escaped with nothing worse than a few cuts and bruises.

Within the year this same captain took off in darkness in a York from Natal bound for Rio de Janeiro. As the aircraft built up speed along the runway the tread of one tyre detached itself and still flailing around was brought into the housing in the inboard engine nacelle as the undercarriage was retracted. The crew had felt some wheel vibration and when a reasonable altitude was gained the undercarriage was extended and the first officer went aft to examine the wheel as best he could from the passenger cabin. In the darkness it seemed that there was a patch of oil on one wheel when in fact he was looking at the only portion of the tread that remained. The undercarriage was retracted again and the flight was continued towards Rio de Janeiro. Unfortunately the flailing tread had destroyed the proper functions of the engine's oil supply and after a while the propeller revolutions increased far beyond the normal range and could not be stopped and "feathered". Within minutes the engine caught fire and this could not be extinguished. The captain attempted to land at the small military airfield at Caravelas, overshot the field in the darkness and crashed in rough ground beyond. There were several fatalities amongst the passengers.

In his book *Three dimensional darkness* Captain Lincoln Lee, himself a former B.S.A.A. pilot, wrote that an airline was reluctant to employ an unlucky pilot and he may well have had this man in mind. He resigned from our company and was engaged as a first officer by another where he was given to understand that he could expect a command in due time, subject to satisfactory performance of his duties. In fact he did not obtain a command, the airline management no doubt believing that if he was involved in a third disaster there would inevitably be a reflection, however unwarranted, upon them for employing him.

More fortunate was Captain John Wright taking off from Lima's old airport Limatambo. His York also unravelled the tread from a tyre as it built up speed along the runway. Aware that something was seriously retarding the take off but committed to an attempt to climb away as the obstructions beyond the runway loomed before him he felt the aircraft wheels strike a low wall as he began the ascent. Wright knew that he must fly around to use as much fuel as possible before he returned for a belly landing. The Yorks had no fuel jettison system. It was a fine Sunday and he told the control tower that it would

Firemen around Avro York after a wheels up landing, Lima.                    *J. Wright*

be a few hours before the aircraft would be lightened enough for a landing. He asked for full crash facilities, fire tenders and ambulances to be alerted. In no time the news was flashed over Lima's radio stations and the Peruvians in a procession of cars drove out to the airport and its perimeter roads to watch this unusual event. At one point the controller asked what the crew were doing. "We are all having tea at present," came the reply and this in turn was passed by Lima radio to an enthralled audience. The aircraft finally made a perfect belly landing and was covered in foam by the fire tenders. No one was hurt and the fuselage so little damaged that after repairs the York was flown away a few weeks later. The President of Peru had a gold medal struck for the captain who had to make a special return trip to Lima for an official presentation.

An interesting experiment was being carried out at this time by Flight Refuelling Ltd., the company formed by Sir Alan Cobham, with a tanker Lancastrian operating from Santa Maria airport in the Azores. B.S.A.A. had a Lancastrian equipped for in-flight refuelling and some direct flights from London to Bermuda were successfully intercepted and refuelled in the air. The Tudors which were about to be introduced had an operating range no better than the Lancastrians which they were to replace and an in-flight refuelling operation was being considered to avoid stops at Dakar and the Azores. However subsequent events overtook any such plan.

# CHAPTER FOUR

# "Star Tiger" is Missing

I FLEW as a first officer on the Tudor IV on several flights to the Caribbean. It had soon become apparent that it did not really have the range to operate from the Azores to Bermuda, a distance of about two thousand nautical miles. There was insufficient information of the direction and strength of the upper winds at the altitudes at which we intended to fly the Tudor and the meteorology office at Santa Maria invariably produced forecasts of winds very much lighter than the very strong westerlies which we regularly encountered.

The flight from London to the Azores took about seven hours and after a refuelling stop the same crew were sometimes airborne for a further fourteen hours en route to Bermuda. A look at the map of the western Atlantic will show Bermuda far from any alternative airfield in the event of bad weather. Therefore we carried an "island reserve" of not less than ninety minutes fuel for holding in the event of bad weather preventing an immediate landing upon our arrival overhead the airfield. It is true that Bermuda seldom has a very low cloud base or poor visibility but very strong winds and rain are not uncommon. One of our Lancastrians once circled for as long as it was able while waiting for a storm to abate. The storm had extinguished many of the runway and airfield lights and flooded portions of the runway. Finally obliged to attempt a landing, the Lancastrian pilot touched down heavily on the flooded runway and the aircraft suffered severe damage.

Tudor flights from the Azores would climb up and level out at their chosen flight level, perhaps twenty-two thousand feet. The navigator had only the stars to guide him. There was no bubble astrodome but a tough thick optical flat surface which distorted the star one chose to sight unless one could stand so as to place the star in the centre of the glass. It was very difficult to obtain the desired small "cocked hat" astro fix in circumstances where one stood holding the sextant in lifted arms, legs straddled to counteract the motion of the aircraft. On our older aircraft the sextant had been suspended from a hook at the centre of the astrodome and one had only to guide and steady it.

With the passing of each hour the crew became increasingly tired. The two pilots could take it in turn to close their eyes but there was only one radio officer and the responsibility for navigation on the sector rested upon one man.

After the aircraft had passed the point of no return much stronger winds were often encountered. Alarmed at the probable disappearance of their "island reserve" fuel, pilots usually descended to lower levels in the hope of minimising the strong headwinds but this meant descending into or below the cloud and the navigator had little further opportunity to obtain a position from star sighting. Thus the flight continued on dead reckoning with no certain knowledge of drift or ground speed.

This dire situation occurred several times and on one occasion a captain alerted the air-sea rescue service of the U.S. Air Force at Kindley airfield in Bermuda. An aircraft flew out and intercepted the Tudor. The crew were accurately advised of their bearing and distance from Bermuda. Just enough fuel remained. Vastly relieved but disconcerted by the impression likely to be made on his passengers by the sight of the lifeboat equipped rescue aircraft flying alongside him the captain asked the American pilot to fly a little way behind and out of their sight. He was no less embarrassed when the American crew in their startling "rescue" clothing came cheerfully into the canteen where crew and passengers were assembled to discuss the successful mission.

Various stratagems were attempted to ensure an arrival at Bermuda with a safe margin of fuel. Some captains flew from London to Keflavik in Iceland, thence to Gander with a third stage to Bermuda. Others flew to the Azores and decided whether to attempt a direct flight to Bermuda on the evidence of the latest reports of upper winds. If in doubt the flight was routed first to Gander and continued to Bermuda after refuelling. It was not unknown for captains to leave behind members of the crew such as the second officer and second stewardess in order to carry more fuel. At least one romance blossomed from such an occasion but a steward who spent three weeks in Iceland before he was picked up by another aircraft did not appreciate his enforced holiday and tendered his resignation.

On one of the occasions when I was flying the Tudor we taxied out from London Airport and during our engine run prior to take off we found that we could not obtain the full range of pitch control on one of the propellers. The captain decided to taxi from the runway over the short distance to the B.S.A.A. hangar. "Nip out and find Wilbur Wright," he ordered. "Bring him on board and let him decide if this is good enough." The passengers watched with curiosity and no doubt some apprehension as I hurried aft, opened the main door at the rear of the aircraft and jumped to the ground. Wilbur Wright was the company's chief of engineering. He appeared swiftly and scrambled up into the aircraft, following me into the cockpit. A few moments later we were surprised to find that A.V.M. Bennett had also come aboard. He had watched the Tudor taxi out and then make its way from the runway to the maintenance area and had driven across the airport to the aircraft. He and Wright decided that the propeller control was serviceable and left us, nodding and smiling reassuringly at the bewildered passengers. We took off for Lisbon shortly thereafter but en route the weather at Lisbon and our alternate airport deteriorated and the captain decided to return to London. Preparing to land we found ourselves unable to extend the undercarriage. We flew around the airport whilst attempts were made to obtain the three green lights that would confirm that the wheels were down and locked. We were reluctant to use the final resort, the emergency air bottle system, because we had been instructed that this involved many hours of subsequent work by the ground engineers. Finally the captain asked the tower controller to ring Wilbur Wright and tell him that failing any bright ideas we were going to use the emergency system. By this time quite a few aircraft were stacked above us. "Wilbur Wright says go ahead," we were told. The other pilots in the area could be forgiven for wondering what sort of aircraft we were flying. At any rate the system worked properly and the wheels locked down.

With the delivery of some Tudors and the expansion of services early in 1948, including one to Havana, I was promoted to a command on the Yorks and Lancastrians. I reported to the new B.S.A.A. head office off St James Street in London for an interview which I remember very well. The Company's unhappy accident record must have weighed very heavily on the operations manager's mind. Always a most charming man he told me that absolute safety must be the watchword in future and every decision I made must have safety in mind. The Company simply could not afford any further disasters. Of those who were being considered for command I seemed the least desperate choice but I was urged to decline if I felt inadequate to accept the responsibility. Then aged twenty-six and with three and a half thousand hours in the air I cheerfully accepted the opportunity offered.

Everyone was always kept busy in B.S.A.A. For the crews there were no long breaks between trips and flying has always been an occupation that plays havoc with the accepted criteria in most walks of life; that the family spend Christmas together, a husband takes his wife out on their wedding anniversary and tries to be home early for the children's birthday parties. In the airlines one can consider oneself lucky to be home at all on these occasions and it is quite an achievement for the husband to be available to congratulate his wife on the birth of a child. Given nine months notice I applied for my annual leave in order to be on hand for just such an event but babies, like so many aircraft prototypes, are not always forthcoming on the scheduled delivery date. The whole of my two weeks leave went by and I had to plead for a week of "duty crew" to remain in the country for a little longer. Still nothing. Our family doctor said that he had never lost a father yet and urged me on my way: I was in Dakar southbound when I received the cable with the good news of my daughter's birth. No real solution to the problem of an individual's private commitments has been found nor is it likely to be. In recent years a "bidding" system based entirely on seniority has resulted in about a fifth of the pilots being able to arrange their work pattern fairly closely to what they want whilst the rest take pot luck with whatever is left over.

Passengers complained bitterly at the noisiness in the Yorks but quickly discovered that the rear passenger cabin was less deafening. I remember being surprised and curious

The author (centre) with crew members in a Dakar, Senegal, cafe.

The author (at right) with a B.S.A.A. York crew.

when one solitary passenger, a well-known Peer of the Realm, voluntarily chose to sit in the empty forward cabin. I wondered whether he was already stone deaf. During the night he rang for the stewardess who had to lean nearer and nearer to him to try and hear what he wanted. This became apparent when he grabbed her and it was a minute or so before she was able to break free and hurry into the cockpit to complain to me. I went back with her and switched on the forward cabin lights to illuminate this podgy rather ridiculous-looking man blinking in the sudden glare.

"I've been a very naughty fellow," he confessed meekly and I had difficulty in expressing my disapproval in suitably serious tones: however, we left the lights on for the remainder of the night. Passenger behaviour in the Yorks and other Merlin-engined aircraft often astonished the crews and many of us attributed their activities to the continuous vibration of the very high revolutions of Rolls-Royce engines.

The entry into service of the Tudors was intended to restore our competitive position amongst the other airline who were replacing the Douglas DC4 with the pressurised DC6 or Lockheed Constellations. Initially the Tudors went into service across the mid-Atlantic to the Caribbean and down the west coast of South America, gradually replacing the Lancastrian. When more Tudors were delivered the airline intended to replace the Yorks also and become an all-Tudor fleet. In another two years the delivery of the first Comet I was anticipated. Provided that the airline's operating set-backs were behind us the future looked very bright. The huge Princess flying boat was also being considered and I had carried a team from the Ministry of Civil Aviation to South America to examine prospective landing sites. The spirits of the small number that made up B.S.A.A. were very high and so were our hopes, but once again disaster struck.

50

A view of the Andes mountains from an Avro Tudor.                    *British Airways*

One night a Lancastrian was flying from the Azores to Bermuda and the Tudor "Star Tiger" was following in its wake, some way behind but maintaining radio contact with it. The Tudor had encountered strong head winds at altitude and the captain conferred with his colleague in the Lancastrian who confirmed the winds and reported that he had already descended to a lower altitude for this reason. No trouble was reported by the Tudor crew and radio contact between the pilots was maintained until the Lancastrian pilot advised that he was about to descend into Bermuda. The Tudor did not arrive over the island at its expected time nor did the control tower make contact with it. This had happened before and at first no alarm was raised. As the hours went by it became obvious that the Tudor could not now be expected to land at Bermuda or anywhere else except in the ocean and at daybreak a full scale search of the area was set in train. No trace of the aircraft, no wreckage or liferaft was found.

In London the inevitable emergency conferences considered what had happened and a decision had to be taken whether one isolated accident to a Tudor justified the grounding of the type. Sabotage might have been the cause. The aircraft was known to have been flying much lower than usual. Control might have been lost in a severe storm or the barometric pressure might have shown the aircraft to have been higher than it really was and consequently it flew into the sea. The combustion chamber of the cabin heating system was also suspect. Before a decision was taken to continue passenger services there was some acrimony between the Minister for Civil Aviation and Air Vice Marshal Bennett and statements to the newspapers by the latter without consultation with the other members of the board of B.S.A.A. led to a crisis. Bennett was dismissed.

The Russian blockade of West Berlin was in effect at this time and Bennett wasted no time in putting two Tudors fitted as tankers into the airlift to the city. His newly formed company "Fairflight" also operated charters to the Middle and Far East and as he frequently piloted a Tudor himself I met him on one or two occasions "down the route". Then he wound up his Company after the loss of a Tudor with all on board on the approach to a small airfield in Wales. Bennett has always been a supremely patriotic man and throughout his time in B.S.A.A. always inspired the staff to work long hours to keep the aircraft flying. His personal enthusiasm and commitment would not indefinitely have overcome the increasing union influence in the airlines but it was the calamity of successive accidents which had brought matters to a head. I did not meet him again until about twenty years later when he was a guest of B.O.A.C. on the inaugural VC10 flight to Israel which I commanded. He spent some time on the flight deck and asked questions about the new "Doppler" navigation equipment so that he could bring up to date the latest edition of his own publication *The Complete Air Navigator.*

To replace him in B.S.A.A. Air Commodore Brackley was brought in from B.O.A.C. where he had been Joint Vice Chairman with Mr Whitney Straight. His tenure of office was tragically short. Setting off on an inspection of our routes he was drowned whilst bathing from the famous Copacabana beach at Rio de Janeiro.

The existence of B.S.A.A. was now almost at an end, but not before a second Tudor disaster. This time "Star Ariel" had taken off from Bermuda bound for Nassau and its last message reported that it had reached cruising altitude. The weather on the route was believed to be good but the Tudor never reached Nassau and the subsequent search failed to reveal any debris on the ocean's surface. On the day that morning newspapers carried headlines of this latest misfortune I was travelling in uniform to London Airport in a Green Line bus from Chalfont St Peter where I lived. I had been detailed for flying practice on a Tudor and had left my home before looking at my own newspaper. The bus was full and I was standing. I paid no particular notice to the curious stares of some of the passengers until I glanced down at the newspaper one of them was holding and read what had happened.

All the usual theories were aired yet again with an additional one—"metal fatigue". In a highly entertaining novel which had just been published, *No Highway* by Nevil Shute, the crash of a new airliner had been attributed to metal fatigue and the author's own background in the aviation industry, together with his popular following as a superb storyteller, ensured wide publicity for this theory. The complete absence of any clues to the loss of either aircraft caused it to be grounded from passenger service. Later it was cleared for unpressurised flying after a number of modifications had been made to some of the systems. As a long range passenger airliner the Tudor was finished. With our Yorks and Lancastrians B.S.A.A. could not hope to compete against the Constellations and DC6s of our rivals.

B.O.A.C. were about to take delivery of the new Argonauts and faint hopes existed for a time among us that some of these could be diverted to B.S.A.A. Despite all that had happened we still hoped to continue as a separate airline but the decision was taken by the government to merge the company with B.O.A.C. The ensuing dismay among the staff even took the form of a protest meeting in Caxton Hall where a few embarrassed individuals having been proposed and seconded by general acclaim were instructed to lobby Members of Parliament in support of our case. This came to naught and in the next few months the Argonauts and Constellations of B.O.A.C. took over our routes to South America and we were required to replace the badges and brevets on our uniforms.

All this was over twenty years ago and I recall most clearly the strong loyalty and keenness of everyone in B.S.A.A. In return for a very small salary prodigious hours were worked by those in the hangars as well as in the air. Of course in a small airline everyone knows everyone else and there is less tendency to blame that shadowy body "them" when anything went wrong. Yet one is entitled to ask whether blame could be attributed anywhere for the numerous accidents that had befallen the company and to try and account for them. B.O.A.C. were a much larger organisation and they too operated Yorks and Lancastrians but proportionately they had had far fewer crashes. Many of their captains were former Imperial Airways pilots but, as in B.S.A.A., a great number had been engaged with almost immediate commands as they were released by R.A.F. squadrons on demobilisation or secondment. It is probable that the leavening of older pilots inculcated a stronger sense of caution on their younger colleagues from the R.A.F.

I remember a radio officer in B.S.A.A., one of several such men, older than most of us, who had been at sea before entering aviation. He told me that he had been on an aircraft which diverted from Rio de Janeiro when the airport "went out" in heavy rain and low scudding cloud. The captain had briefed the crew on his intentions. "I'll have a look at the military airfield on the coast south of the bay," he had said, "and there may be enough fuel to reach Vittoria although no one in the control tower there speaks English. Failing that it will have to be the beach." The radio officer was horrified. "This is a civil airline, isn't it?" he demanded urgently; "civil for Christ's sake. There are far too many bloody heroes in this outfit if you ask me."

I can recall take-offs at top weight from Natal to cross the South Atlantic when the oil and cylinder head temperatures were verging on their maximum permitted level, and the oil pressures sometimes as low as one could allow before being expected to shut the engine down. Yet if any blame is attributed for this state of affairs one must ask if we were operating a suitable aircraft for the job at all, bearing in mind the "state of the art", the general knowledge of aviation at that time.

In B.S.A.A. we were frequently dismayed by the weather through which we flew to reach our destinations but seldom did anyone turn back. If one did would it be any better the next day and what if other flights had continued unconcerned? The "press on" spirit was always much in evidence. The lesson to be learnt was that courage and a determination to keep on flying were incompatible with the ultimate requirement of safety. The "heroic era" of aviation had to be allowed to lapse if airline salesmen were to lure passengers from ships and buses and trains.

Any study of the accident record of B.S.A.A. in its short life must horrify anyone today but it is a fact that in the first few years after the war the general accident record among commercial airlines in both Europe and the United states was appalling. It was a time when many small airlines with inadequate capital and resources operated for a short while and then failed. Neither sufficient aircraft or finances were spared for crew training. There were so many accidents to the Douglas Dakotas that even this superb aircraft, still to be seen flying today, was the subject of ill-informed comment in the press. Whilst there were some pilots flying without a proper understanding of the effects of ice on the wings and without adequate maps showing the hazards of high ground along the routes they were operating, there were also airports insufficiently equipped with runway and approach lighting and with weak medium frequency radio beacons as a landing aid or none at all. Nevertheless the record of B.S.A.A. attracted adverse comment in the House of Commons. The arrival at Bermuda of Tudors with tiny reserves of fuel had not escaped the notice of the Governor of the island and he had made representations to appropriate quarters in Whitehall. A debate on civil aviation in the Commons ventilated the unhappy history of the Company and whilst there were those who rose to our defence they were very few. The merger and the extinction of B.S.A.A. was approved.

As a first officer I had been fortunate to fly with careful competent captains. I had obtained my command within a year and had had no particularly alarming experiences but I do recollect one humiliating episode. I had delayed overnight in Rio de Janeiro owing to the weather and set off the following day for Dakar with a transit stop at Natal. At dawn I descended towards the coast of Senegal and as the shoreline came hazily into view the tower operator reported no other traffic and a light and variable wind. "I have you in sight. You are clear to land straight ahead." No invitation could have been more welcome after such a long spell of duty and peering forward I saw a runway, called for the landing check and full flaps and shortly thereafter made a perfect landing. Unfortunately I had arrived at the adjoining military airfield whose existence I had overlooked because it was never illuminated at night when our services were normally scheduled through Dakar. I took off again and landed minutes later at Dakar's civil airport and endured caustic and ribald comment for some considerable time thereafter.

Throughout the years this sort of mistake has not been uncommon, but its likelihood has been partly eliminated by orders to pilots to carry out a real or simulated instrument approach on every possible occasion, tuning in an approach beacon whenever available in line with the runway in use. Failing any such beacon great caution must be exercised, especially when landing into the sun as one can be misled by landmarks. Even London Airport has been missed by a few pilots who have touched down at Northolt. A landing to the south-west at London Airport is comparatively rare as most pilots elect to land on the longer east-west runway unless the cross wind component is too great. The control tower instruct pilots to call over the gasometer on final approach but there is another gasometer to the north and aircraft flying over that see Northolt's runway before them. Eventually the letters NO were painted on this second gasometer. There have been other main airports with pitfalls for the unwary but most became well known to the initiated. Beirut once had a minor airfield which was being visited by a team from a company considering its suitability for their twin-engined Vickers Viking. Their deliberations on the adequacy of the runway length were settled when a four-engined aircraft approached and landed: whereupon the pilot realised his error, turned the aircraft and took off in the opposite direction.

# CHAPTER FIVE

# B.O.A.C. Again—The Argonauts

THE pilots of B.S.A.A. were not welcomed with open arms by our colleagues in B.O.A.C., many of whom felt that our standard of operating would bring no credit at all to the senior corporation. We had been generously accorded our existing ranks and seniority and this caused a long jam on promotion which was to be felt for a very considerable number of years. B.O.A.C. already had enough pilots and the influx of those whom B.S.A.A. had engaged additionally to fly cargo-carrying Tudors on the Berlin airlift, which had recently come to an end, further aggravated the problem of over-establishment. Pilots who had joined B.O.A.C. in 1946 or earlier had quickly obtained commands. From 1947 onwards there were many who were to wait fifteen years or more before at last promotion came.

Most of us were now posted to the "Argonaut" flight and this aircraft was used by B.O.A.C. to operate the route across the south Atlantic to the east coast of South America and to Santiago. Twenty-two of these aircraft were delivered to B.O.A.C. and they were progressively introduced on routes to the Middle East, the Far East including Japan and to all parts of Africa. The Argonaut was basically a Douglas DC4 but with a pressurised hull and with similar Rolls-Royce engines to those of the Tudor. It was easier to taxi because it was steered by a nosewheel and both the pressurisation and the cabin heating were superior to that of the Tudor. A periscopic sextant in a roof mounting displaced the old hand-held Mark IX. The aircraft was built by Canadair Ltd under licence to Douglas. The Merlin engines with their high cruising r.p.m. made it very noisy but an improvement was achieved by a cross-over system whereby the engine exhaust stubs were all located outboard of each engine in relation to the fuselage. Initially there were troubles with over-high engine temperatures and a fluctuation of pitch at a certain stage in the climb but these problems were quickly overcome. In due course the Argonaut became the principal workhorse of B.O.A.C. for seven years and it was to be about ten years before it ceased to carry the Corporation's passengers. Two were destroyed in accidents during that time.

I recollect one unusual fault that developed on very few occasions. A small panel on the underside of the aircraft hull could be opened on the ground to permit the lavatories to be emptied. Once in a while one of these came adrift in flight. The unfortunate person seated in that lavatory found himself fulfilling the same function as the legendary boy who stemmed the flow from the hole in the dyke. I was reliably informed that some considerable effort was required to prise oneself free. The loss of pressurisation was then quickly stemmed by the lid slamming firmly down over the seat. Nerveracking for the victim but we lost no one in that way.

I have mentioned that the block in promotion had not endeared us to our B.O.A.C. colleagues but it was not long before the natural affinity among all pilots overcame the initial barriers. At first when we reported for a flight there was a tendency to look at one's crew and count "two of us, three of them" but time eliminated this. The radio officers also settled down quickly. Our Stargirls had to accustom themselves to working under the authority of a steward but they were a fine lot of girls and the B.O.A.C. crews were quick to express their approval. "I reserve judgment on you lot," one B.O.A.C. captain told me "but at least you brought some magnificent girls with you." A smaller number of B.S.A.A. pilots went to the Constellation flight which took over the mid-Atlantic services to the Caribbean and west coast of South America. One of our senior pilots, Captain Rodley, was chosen to join the development flight to prepare for the introduction of the Comet I.

In 1949 the headquarters of B.O.A.C. was the former office of the engineering firm Simmonds Accessories on the Great West Road and was colloquially known as the "Nuthouse" to the staff. In a few years time H.Q. was to move again to the present site on London Airport where it has always been called the "Kremlin". In B.S.A.A. we had reported at London Airport one and a half hours before take off but now we had to fall in with B.O.A.C.'s rule of two and a half hours during which time a meal was available if required. This lengthy period also enabled a stand-by crew member to be summoned if someone failed to report at the correct time.

There was also a rule against drinking in uniform in any public place, even after completion of all flying duties. This was not so surprising when one appreciated what a small proportion of the world's population actually travelled by air and the apprehension and nervousness of many who had still to be convinced that flying was safe. One incident perfectly illustrates how necessary it is for flight crews to exercise discretion.

A camera crew were busy at London Airport shooting sequences for a film called "Out of the Clouds" in which actors and actresses played B.O.A.C. staff. The late James Robertson Justice was perfectly cast as a very senior captain. But while he waited for a summons to appear before the cameras he decided to quench his thirst among the passengers in the airport bar. Before long a stream of anxious travellers besieged the B.O.A.C. ticket desk to protest that if the pilot with the beard was their captain they did not propose to fly with him.

Accordingly crew members usually collected together in a hotel bedroom to have a drink after flying and before they went to bed. Alternatively the hotel bar might suddenly be invaded by a group in identical white shirts, black ties and navy blue trousers, only a disparity in jackets to disguise the nature of their calling. These were the days when newspapers were not put on board for passengers to read if they carried a report of an air disaster and on such occasions it was customary for a gang of men to paint out the company's emblem and name from the fuselage.

There was still the unpopular task of duty crew but it came round less often. Whereas in B.S.A.A. we had collected our own weather folders from the meteorology office and worked out the flight plan ourselves, now we found an entire department of operations officers who were scattered at every stop along the routes who did this for us. The numbers on the ground proportional to the number of aircraft were very high. Each aircraft fleet was then self-accounting and the Argonaut manager deplored the expense and had instructed his navigators not to accept the prepared flight plans and to work out their own. This gesture was over-ruled by his superiors. Gradually over the years the captain's freedom of choice of route and flight level has eroded but mainly due to the sheer weight of traffic on the principal air routes. In 1947 we had learned a method of "best time track" navigation called pressure pattern flying which involved a sensible interpretation of the isobars at various cruising levels. Few can ever have had the opportunity to practise it.

Now therefore we reported much earlier at London Airport but with much less to do before we took off and a captain had literally to bundle the navigator out of his seat if he wished to keep current his own navigation licence. Airport facilities for a good instrument approach throughout the new routes on which we found ourselves were as sadly lacking as those we had known before. A year or two later aircraft were progressively fitted with the instrument landing system (I.L.S.) but meanwhile London Airport introduced the ground controlled approach (G.C.A.). A small team of men under a controller observed the aircraft's movements on radar screens and having talked the pilot down to the threshold of the runway finally told him to "look ahead and land". I was always most impressed by their great skill and the calm clearly spoken economy of words they used. We often had cause to be very grateful for this service which is still available today but there were then some pilots who were uneasy about surrendering all responsibility for avoiding high terrain or obstacles to a man on the ground who through human error or lack of expertise might steer them into danger.

In 1949 some British pilots were still fighting a rearguard action to preserve their complete freedom for decision-making in the air but airlines were anxious to avoid the type of accident that occurred when a pilot was determined to attempt a landing at an airport despite negligible visibility. Accordingly many companies began to publish minimum ceiling and visibility conditions for each runway on every airport that might be used, defining the conditions in accordance with the type of instrument facility being used. No reasonable pilot can regret this. It has protected everybody. Today there are different rules in every country. In Britain the Civil Aviation Authority takes upon itself the responsibility for declaring to an approaching pilot the visibility or runway visual range. The cloud base found by the pilot will not be contested but he must accept the visual range reported to him and may not insist that, as the runway is clearly visible for a mile or more before him, he intends to land. The reason for this is the danger from very low lying fog which is invisible to the pilot until he crosses the runway threshold and is on the point of flare when suddenly the ground, lights and all his visual clues disappear from sight.

Some years were still to pass before any legal flight time limitations were laid down. As in B.S.A.A. and most international companies very long spells of duty were assigned to crews. The pilots' representatives would occasionally protest at some schedules and the management would enumerate the particular costs of establishing a slip crew at a suggested place on the route. Sometimes the obvious place for a slip might be so extremely unpopular with crews owing to the climate, location, or standard of accommodation available that both parties accepted an unsatisfactory schedule. Nevertheless we often flew for much too long a spell particularly when delays of several hours occurred for mechanical reasons or waiting for the weather to improve. There were a number of pilots who being young, fit and intensely enthusiastic overlooked the effect of lack of sleep upon their judgment and competence. Accidents to a flying boat landing at Bahrain and a Constellation at Singapore, both fully airworthy and operating in good weather conditions were attributed in part to the fatigue of the pilots. Both flights had been behind schedule and in one case the captain had attempted to make up time by eliminating a scheduled rest stop.

The older pilots were as competent as their juniors in holding their height and flying a course in cloud and in turbulence but in the days when no radio direction-finding aids had been provided many had become accustomed to devising their own system for descent and approach to airfields shrouded in mist or low cloud. The old hand, explaining as he flew, would catechise his un-instructed co-pilot. "Keep that peak on your port side, steer south and you can safely descend to two hundred feet over the sea. Now bank round to starboard and roll out on a heading of 045 degrees. Watch for a tall white building on the coast. Fly over that and follow the railway line for four miles, keeping it on your port side. You should see the hangar and windsock any moment now."

With an exact knowledge of the terrain, an appreciation of when to admit defeat and the wit to know how to climb out of danger the veterans had earned for their airlines a reputation for regularity of schedule keeping in fair weather and foul. On the Argonaut flight there were several captains who had once been based at Hong Kong's Kaitak Airport which lay in a bay alongside mountains and hills. They prided themselves on arrivals at the airport when others had not even made the attempt.

In the future the airline pilot was going to have to operate into too many airports to be able to possess an adequate knowledge of local features. Modern technology was slowly providing electronic means to enable him to practise more sophisticated approach techniques. Moreover the increasing number of aircraft using the airports did not permit the local air traffic controller to welcome pilots performing their own personal brand of approach and descent towards a congested space.

The Ministry of Civil Aviation was well aware that standards of licensing and operating needed urgently to be improved and by 1950 every pilot holding a licence to carry passengers was required to take a further practical examination in an aircraft to demonstrate his ability to fly accurately on instruments and to conduct a safe descent down to minimum limits using an approach aid like the Standard Beam or Radio Range which were currently in use. Today pilots must submit to checks upon their competency every six months. Their ability to fly on instruments and to handle every emergency is under particular scrutiny. The checks are conducted either by government inspectors or by the airline's own instructors who are licensed by the Civil Aviation Authority. Additionally every captain is checked by an inspector once a year in the course of an ordinary service flight.

I flew the Argonaut from 1950 to 1957 and such was the extensive pattern of the routes which it served that I did not even in all that time fly to all of the points where the aircraft was operated. Partly this was due to the system in force whereby the captain in command of a scheduled service was required by the regulations to be thoroughly conversant with airports on his route. To avoid the time and expense of sending the captains on preliminary visits to every airfield B.O.A.C. kept us on a limited number of routes.

The very first service on which I flew an Argonaut was under the supervision of another captain to Calcutta. I had been stationed there during the war when I had been flying over the "Hump" to China. We landed en route at Rome, Cairo, Bahrain and Karachi. It was at Cairo where the crew "slipped" that I first encountered the curious B.O.A.C. system whereby the captain was accommodated separately from the remainder of the crew. It was never an inflexible rule and I believe that it only originated at the end of the war when the former Imperial Airways captains expressed a preference to be lodged apart from the more youthful members of their crew in their leisure time abroad. The practice lingered on for many years but eventually was modified into an arrangement whereby the operating crew were accommodated in one hotel and the cabin crew at another. Even so there were numerous stations where the whole crew remained together and it certainly facilitated pick up arrangements by crew buses.

I made many visits to Rome on the Argonaut flight and as this lovely city became a regular "slip" station for the crews I came to know it well and developed an abiding interest in wine. The oil-producing state of Kuwait was another place where we landed. The landing strip was marked out in huge daubs of black oil on the hard-packed sand. In 1950 there was no airfield control tower or even one building. Only daylight arrivals were authorised and it was necessary first to circle the airfield to observe the windsock before deciding in which direction to land. There was one tent for passenger handling and business was brisk. A valuable shipment of gold or silver was met by a troop of white-robed Arabs armed with long old-fashioned rifles and bandoliers of ammunition across their chests. Having collected their consignment they would depart in a cloud of dust across the sands to the small town where I once observed an executed man swinging on gallows in the main square. Today the town has a Hilton hotel and a modern highway connects it to the new airport.

Sheikhs of high and low rank have for many years been good and valued customers of B.O.A.C. and sometimes shown great generosity to the crews. Pilots might be offered a gold watch or cigarette case, but as aviation has become more commonplace such happenings are rare today.

We had one solitary representative at Kuwait and he was responsible for passenger handling. No engineer or spare parts were available. One day I prepared to start the engines after a routine transit stop and discovered that a starter motor had failed. It would be impossible to start one of the engines. There were about twenty passengers on board whose destination was Bahrain. Fortunately for them there was a Dakota on the airstrip whose crew were willing and ready to take them on the remaining lap of their journey. This Dakota and its crew were normally occupied carrying oil company staff on local flights and also brought in fresh vegetables and fruit from as far afield as Beirut.

One of my passengers was Air Commodore Whittle, who can justly claim to be responsible for making Britain pre-eminent in the early introduction of the jet engine which he had successfully pioneered. When I explained to the passengers that the Argonaut was indefinitely delayed but that they would be able to continue their flight on the Dakota he surprised me by offering an alternative suggestion. "Leave us on the ground," he said. "Then with an empty aircraft you ought to be able to get airborne on the three good engines. The fourth will windmill and can be restarted in the air. Land again and pick up."

There is no doubt that it could have been done but those who operate civil aircraft, those who insure them and those who license the pilots do not encourage such extreme solutions to temporary problems. The passengers looked far from disappointed when I turned the suggestion down. They were fortunate to continue on their way so rapidly. The crew and aircraft remained at Kuwait for three days before our spare part arrived from London.

As far back as 1950 B.O.A.C. were carrying parties of schoolchildren at the beginning and end of the school terms. The Middle East oil-producing countries were then the principal source of this revenue. Anxious parents would see off their tearful offspring and for a time we would be flying with the most subdued lot of children one ever saw. Not for long. Air sickness bags would be converted into masks with slits for their eyes. Pillow fights would follow. Occasionally a desperate steward would beg the captain to come aft and bark stern commands for order. At such times I always spared a thought for those worried parents who no doubt pictured their children in continued misery.

When Argonaut aircraft replaced the Hermes I made my first visit to East Africa. It had been the custom of the flying boat pilots, when they had served this route, to fly quite low over the areas where game could be seen and around such natural attractions as Murchison Falls. With aircraft cruising at much higher levels this sort of diversion was becoming less common but occasionally when we were ahead of schedule we descended early and flew around the Falls.

Kenya in 1950 was suffering the Mau Mau rebellion and murders and atrocities were reported almost daily in the newspapers. Nairobi was then rather like a frontier town and the two hotels, the *Norfolk* and the *New Stanley,* were more commonly patronised by the European settlers than the air tourist of today. These visitors arrived dusty or mud-bespattered depending upon the season and all of them carried a revolver. It was not thought necessary to issue firearms to our crews but the Very pistol and cartridges were removed from aircraft on overnight stops to avoid their theft.

The *Norfolk* hotel has changed little but the *New Stanley,* famed for its long bar, has since been reconstituted as a modern concrete block. One recollection of that period was the fury of B.O.A.C. crews at being woken at six o'clock in the morning, the normal routine call of the hotels. Their regular guests must have been a spartan breed. The hotels did not then provide "Do not disturb" signs and those constructed by desperate sleepers were ignored. If necessary the room boy who had brought tea tapped the spoon against the cup a few inches from one's ear.

Eastleigh airport was then in use. It did not possess a modern runway. Before take off or landing care had to be taken to ensure that the red earth had not been reduced to treacle by the rains. In the dry season our propellers unleashed a temporary sandstorm.

Nairobi has remained a favourite stopping place for me. With its game reserve, sports facilities and attractive trees and flowers, the strong sunshine but cool evenings, it is not surprising that visitors are today arriving in Kenya from further and further afield. I also liked Entebbe on Lake Victoria, Uganda, situated precisely on the equator, and I enjoyed playing golf there on the course along the lakeside but it is not for those who prefer towns and cities. East Africa, of course, has its rainy seasons and some pretty stupendous storms build up over Lake Victoria. The approaches to the main runway at Entebbe are made over the lake and the airport commandant has a radio-equipped launch in case of emergency. Occasionally he would take crews out to observe the rhinoceros and to admire the lovely tropical birds occupying the small uninhabited islands on the lake, but all the time the radio would carry news of local aircraft movements.

I made my first flight to Teheran, the capital of Iran, when their prime minister Mossadeq had precipitated the "Abadan crisis" by nationalising the Anglo-Iranian company's petroleum installations. The British government were contemplating a military intervention and B.O.A.C. had been required to assemble York crews in Tripoli equipped with R.A.F. battledress in case it was decided to fly troops to Abadan. Our flight was uneventful but we had instructions to arrive in Teheran with sufficient fuel to return to Tel Aviv and to avoid uplifting fuel if possible. The route Tel Aviv to Teheran has for political

B.O.A.C. Argonaut at Teheran airport, Iran. *British Airways*

reasons required a detour over Turkey to avoid overflying Israel's hostile neighbours Jordan and Syria. The airline captain needs to be very conscious of political susceptibilities in many parts of the world particularly when diverting from one airport to another when weather is bad. The obvious example is the Arab-Israeli problem but from time to time one Arab state is hostile to another one and our Middle East passengers are often anxious about diversions. Bahrain was for many years claimed by Iran and so was not nominated as an alternative for flights routed to Iranian airports, or Iranian airports nominated as alternatives for flights to Bahrain. The Persian Gulf is referred to as the Gulf of Arabia by most of its inhabitants. Occasional outbreaks of strife between India and Pakistan also complicate matters.

There are many parts of the world where stray animals, particularly dogs, are to be found on airfields. West Africa was served by Argonauts when the Hermes was withdrawn and Kano airport in northern Nigeria is an outstanding example. Twenty minutes before an aircraft could be seen or heard a pack of scavenging dogs had not only collected on the airfield but even anticipated the exact spot on which the aircraft could be expected to park. There was always the danger that they would wander on to the runway.

One night I was walking aft through the darkened cabin of my Argonaut when my foot rested upon something soft which emitted a high-pitched yowl. Fearful that I had crushed someone's baby it was some relief to discover that the sufferer was a passenger's small dog. Normally dogs, cats, even rabbits or day-old chicks were carried in the hold along with the cargo but the Argonaut had a small compartment on the flight deck, adjacent to the navigator's seat, in which an overflow of mail or baggage was sometimes stowed. On a flight out of London I found this occupied by a hound of massive proportions, a gift to the Regent of Iraq. The animal stared menacingly at the navigator and, becoming enraged by the noise of the engines, employed all its strength to demolish the box in which it was travelling. The navigator removed himself hastily from the scene and reappeared with the aircraft axe, prepared to defend himself if necessary. To everyone's relief the dog's strength finally ebbed away and the navigator felt able to attend to his duties.

On long journeys dogs were removed from the aircraft at transit stops to be given food and water and allowed to exercise. At Karachi one escaped and the aircraft continued the flight without it. The owner was informed that his dog was often to be seen around the airport but evaded all attempts at recapture. His reply suggested various ways to entice it back but all to no avail. Finally the airline gave the owner a free return ticket to Karachi and he successfully recovered his property.

Less domesticated breeds were carried on York freighters and no one offered to exercise them but a crew approaching their aircraft after an overnight stop halted abruptly when their attention was drawn to a tiger which had taken possession of the captain's seat. One unpopular variety of passenger was the monkey whose smell is rather obnoxious to those forced to share their company.

*　*　*　*　*　*

An Arab horse is led aboard a B.O.A.C. York freighter.

*British Airways*

I often flew to West Africa and the severe line squalls encountered at certain times of the year were a reminder of the weather we had come to respect at similar latitudes over South America. A storm warning radar set would have been most welcome. It was to be a further seven years and the Britannia aircraft before I was to use one. In the line squall season I always dreaded the flight after dusk northbound from Kano, the skies broken over the whole horizon by vivid flashes of lightning. One darkened the cockpit the better to see forward, tightened one's seat harness and peered forward in the hope that as each bright flash momentarily lit up the clouds banked ahead, a less turbulent and more favourable heading would become apparent. Once in a storm there was little one could do except maintain as level an attitude as possible by reference to the artificial horizon and ignore the wild and often contradictory fluctuations of the airspeed indicator, the climb and descent indicator and the altimeter. If one was carried a few thousand feet upward one would expect to come plummeting down soon afterwards. The noise of the rain and hail on the windscreen was matched by the screeching sound of static over the earphones. At night, the propeller tips were illuminated like Catherine wheels and little blue "flames" of St Elmos' fire played about the windscreen.

Airline publicity had heralded the advent of pressurised aircraft with the promise of flying "above the weather" but although one did escape a certain amount of turbulence by flying at twenty instead of ten thousand feet there was still a lot of weather one would have to try and avoid. Generally speaking a pilot had to accept what he found between his point of departure and his destination. Few ever turned back for en-route weather alone if the destination was forecast as having acceptable landing conditions. The pilot can accept poorer weather for a take-off than for a landing. After all he is at the airport. He does not have to find it. Even so each airline has different standards and it still happens that on a foggy day with the airport lounge crowded by delayed passengers, the public address system of most airlines constantly announcing further delays to their flights, one or more airlines will announce that their flights are about to leave.

Soon after the merger of B.S.A.A. with B.O.A.C. a friend of mine was rostered to fly as co-pilot to the veteran Captain O. P. Jones. The latter studied the weather reports with their gloomy forecasts at very considerable length and in complete silence. "Well, Skipper," the co-pilot eventually enquired, "are we going to have a bash?"

"We may go or we may not go," Jones replied severely, "but we will most certainly not have a bash."

One piece of equipment fitted on our aircraft was a primitive form of distance measurement called the Eureka-Rebecca set. It transmitted a pulse to the airport and the responder set on the airfield reacted, presenting the navigator with a blob on his receiver along the ninety mile scale. The airline used these at a number of airports. One was installed at the old civil airport Ciampino near Rome. Pilots arriving at night continually reported that it was not responding but no complaints of malfunction were made by crews during the daytime. The set had been positioned on the roof of the control tower building and the reason for its behaviour was soon discovered. Military personnel were sleeping directly below the roof and its chattering noise when "interrogated" by aircraft had kept them awake: so one of them had been effectively silencing it with a fragment of cardboard stuffed into a vital spot.

Captain O. P. Jones with Sir Arthur Whitten-Brown, transatlantic pioneer of an earlier era.   *British Airways*

# CHAPTER SIX

# The Rise and Fall of the Comet I

SIR Miles Thomas was chairman of B.O.A.C. when the merger had taken place. In addition to the new Argonauts, the Handley Page Hermes had also been introduced on to the routes and the flying boat services were being withdrawn. Although very popular with passengers who liked their spacious seating, the bar and rest cabins, the flying boats had proved extremely expensive to operate and someone had estimated that if B.O.A.C. had paid every intending passenger fifty pounds not to travel the Corporation would have saved money. A year or so later the only reminder of the flying boat era was the continued use of envelopes heavily embossed with the words "at moorings mail" for urgent company messages. In Karachi an old bell had been tolled when the flying boats had touched down. The original inscription on the bell "Imperial Airways" had already been changed to the new name. The old boatman complained that the change had lowered the tone but there was no further use for the bell.

At the time of the merger with B.O.A.C., pilots' check lists were already coming into use and the old memory system of performing the vital actions prior to take off, T.M.P.F.F. or trim, mixture, pitch, fuel, flaps and so forth was discarded. As always there was controversy over this with some instructors insisting that a pilot ought to know the sequence and actions by heart. In the long run the innovation of check lists had to come as aircraft systems became so much more complicated and today the only actions required to be performed without reference to a check list are those in the event of an emergency such as an engine fire, smoke in the cabin or loss of pressurisation. Moreover the check lists have increased to numerous pages of small print. By 1951 there had been some tightening up by the authorities of regulations regarding licences. Both the captain and first officer were required to be fully qualified on the type and only those with the first class navigation licence were navigating across the Atlantic and Indian Oceans.

Nevertheless there was an extraordinary episode when a Hermes took off one night from Tripoli in North Africa southbound across the Sahara to Kano in Nigeria. This was a route where astro-navigation was the primary method of fixing position. Radio beacons were to all practical purposes non-existent. The winds on this route at the height flown by the Hermes are never particularly strong and the skies are usually clear except near Kano in the wet season. The magnetic variation was then one degree at Tripoli and four at Kano. The Hermes had a knob on the navigator's panel enabling him to alter the compass needle to compensate for the change in magnetic variation at appropriate times. One night the officer navigating was a pilot whose practical navigation had always been satisfactory but

The Handley Page Hermes after landing in the western Sahara.                    *C. Houlder*

Passengers and crew around the crashed Hermes.                    *F. Collier*

who had as yet been unable to pass all the academic papers to qualify for the issue of a licence. Although Tripoli-Kano was a long sector and took up to seven hours in a Hermes it did not fall into the oceanic category whereby a qualified navigator was required. The mistake was made of altering the variation knob in stages of ten degrees and not in stages of one degree. The aircraft proceeded on increasingly divergent headings from its proper track with the officer responsible unable to understand why the position lines obtained from sights of stars failed to make any sense when he endeavoured to plot them on his chart. So critical an emergency had arisen when he realised what he had done that an unsuccessful attempt was made to reach an airfield called Atar in Senegal. With fuel almost exhausted the Hermes was put down in the desert and severely damaged on impact with the undulating sand dunes. One crew member died a few days later as a result of injuries but all the others on board were recovered with the assistance of Bedouin tribesmen and a detachment from the French Foreign Legion at Atar.

When the last Hermes and Argonauts had been delivered and the flying boats, Lancastrians, Yorks and Haltons had all been disposed of there were many first officers who saw no prospect of a command for years to come and a number left to take their chance in the charter companies. A very few pilots who were discovered to have combined flying with private trading or smuggling also left but these too we sometimes encountered wearing the uniforms of other airlines. Some of the charter companies were entirely reputable but a few were less so and stories of pilots at the controls for excessively long hours flying aircraft with every manner of defect soon percolated around aviation circles. As companies mushroomed and failed there were pilots who moved from one to another. A few made the reverse journey and came to us, willing to start again on the bottom rung in exchange perhaps for the command of an old bomber converted into a cargo carrier but used for gun-running to one or other of the world's trouble spots.

1952 was the year of Queen Elizabeth's accession to the throne. On Coronation day I watched the first part of the ceremony on television and then reported to the airport for a flight to Tripoli. At the airport helicopters were already arriving with canisters of newsreel film to be flown by R.A.F. Canberra jets to North America and men were to be seen leaping from the helicopters almost before they had touched down and scurrying to waiting aircraft. On the Argonaut we had instructions to offer a glass of champagne to our passengers and it was my duty during the flight to ask them to stand and drink a toast to the new Queen. Almost all those in window seats bumped their heads on the hat racks as they rose. I recollect that I was ordered on no account actually to consume the champagne in my own glass! It was rather a difficult task to perform the ceremony with any dignity on a noisy moving aircraft. It was also often a waste of time to try and capture the jollity of Christmas with a decorated cabin, the traditional pudding and so forth. Foreigners were quite baffled by it. I remember a mother complaining bitterly that her child had almost swallowed a coin in his pudding and the explanation failed to convince her. "Lucky?" she asked. "We don't use your money in our country."

1952 was also the year in which the Comet I was introduced into passenger service. There was enormous public enthusiasm for this aircraft so far in advance of any

De Havilland Comet I. G ALZK.                                              *British Airways*

commercial aircraft then flying or even in development. Its only competitors were the stretched Super-Constellation and the Douglas DC6, both slow piston-engined types. The only other turbine propelled aircraft was the British Viscount recently introduced on short haul routes by B.E.A. In the excitement of Coronation year the British newspapers spoke of the dawn of a new Elizabethan age. All of us in B.O.A.C. envied those who had been chosen to fly the Comet, but the small crew had to work at high pressure. After take-off the first officer climbed out of his seat and assumed responsibility for the navigation and the engineer officer would sometimes move into the vacant co-pilot's seat and assist the captain until the aircraft was ready to descend. Flights were almost always fully booked although only first class passengers were carried.

Many foreign airlines observed the success of the Comet I with great interest but most required a longer range version and the Comet II with Rolls Royce Avon engines in place of de Havilland Ghosts went into production. This version still lacked the range for an acceptable North Atlantic operation but was adequate for the South Atlantic and Panair do

Brasil was one airline which appeared to be a potential buyer. There was talk that de Havilland might fly one to Rio de Janeiro in Panair's colours and Bill Shepherd who had remained in South America to become B.O.A.C.'s manager for the region was worried.

"British companies don't spend enough on advertising out here," he complained to me. "If that aircraft arrives in Panair livery all Brasil will believe it was built in Belo Horizonte by a local engineer called Fernandes." Dejected by the difficulties of winning business for the airline within the confines of a "straight bat" philosophy against the villainies of the competition he railed against the shortcomings of our advertising. "They showed me the proofs; pictures of the Tower of London, Chelsea Flower Show, Henley Royal Regatta. I looked at them all in profound gloom and they sensed my dissatisfaction. One of the advertising men remarked that their firm had been in business for over one hundred years. That gave me my opening. That's exactly the trouble, I told them. You people haven't thought up anything new or original for far too long."

Some pilots are convinced that aviation meteorologists regard it as "infra dig" to look from the windows of their offices at the conditions pertaining outside, preferring to base their forecasts solely on the evidence of their barometers, wet and dry bulb thermometers and other apparatus at their disposal. Those who design aircraft cockpits perhaps think that navigators share this scorn for visual information because they are invariably positioned in the cramped confines behind the pilot, frequently seated with their backs to the aircraft's windscreen.

An interesting attempt by one who hoped to remedy this situation was related to me by John Cunningham, de Havilland chief test pilot. When B.S.A.A. had still been in existence and a probable buyer of the Comet I, Air Vice Marshal Bennett had visited the de Havilland works and put before the designers the particular cockpit layout he thought would most suit the company's requirements. Bennett's thinking reflected his constant concern for the importance of adequate navigational facilities and it was his intention that the navigator should be alongside the captain, ensuring the best possible outward visibility whilst the second pilot was relegated to a rear position.

De Havilland went ahead with the production of a mock-up of the cockpit area embodying these proposals but meanwhile Bennett parted company with B.S.A.A. Time went by and no one came to see the mock up and in due course de Havilland sent a bill for their costs to the airline. This brought the reply that the Board knew nothing about the matter, never having sanctioned any expenditure on such a project, nor would they accept any responsibility for it. Cunningham concluded the tale by remarking that de Havilland's chief accountant became quite apoplectic whenever the subject was discussed.

May 1952 had also seen the introduction of tourist class fares and the Argonaut's interior now carried fifty-six narrow and closely spaced seats. Initially only cold meals were served and breakfast was either tea or coffee with a couple of bread rolls and a packet of sweets. There were insufficient lavatories for so many people and the tasks of the two or three cabin attendants became harder. It had been customary for the captain to walk back and talk to the passengers during the flight and this practice fell into decline from the introduction of tourist, later called economy class. Apart from the narrow aisle and the obstruction caused to the cabin staff who have to move about, the unfortunate captain would often have thrust upon him trays of finished meals, baby's bottles for heating and demands for drinks and other services. To most passengers one uniform is much like another! In the first class cabin with its two abreast seating it was still possible to converse with passengers if one chose a time when the trolleys of food or wines and spirits were not being trundled along the aisle. I am sometimes asked by acquaintances if I ever visit the cabins and talk to passengers and it is amusing to study their expressions when I reply "only the first class" and an explanation is always necessary. Some passengers are delighted to talk to the pilots, others hide behind newspapers or feign sleep and not a few express great concern that one has abandoned one's post or left the controls to some half-trained callow youth. One dear old lady reprimanded me and urged me to go back and "mind the winch or whatever it is". Many passengers ask if they may visit the cockpit and it is a good public relations exercise to accede to requests at convenient times when one is not engaged in constant radio communication or when the navigator needs to use the very confined space to take astro sights. At slack times I am happy to welcome an occasional passenger and the nicest ones stay five minutes and retire. Some overstay their welcome and others misjudge the apparent calm and remark that no one seems to have anything to do. It is impossible to ask forward everyone who asks and crews particularly resent those passengers who enter their "office" uninvited.

At that time captains wore different numbers of gold bands upon their sleeves depending upon their seniority, from two and a half rings for a junior captain to four thick bands for a senior captain, first class. In later years captains of all grades wore four rings because some passengers who had commenced their journey in the charge of an utterly reliable looking grey-haired captain became nervous when a crew change took place and a youthful looking pilot of apparently lower rank assumed command. Today's crews sport a wealth of braid even among the stewards.

After a time those of us flying Argonauts, Constellations and Stratocruisers became aware that our colleagues on the Comet Is had anxieties which we did not share. The Comet I had a small fuel carrying capacity but being a jet consumed fuel voraciously. This meant that when their destination was threatened by bad weather a decision to divert had to be taken in plenty of time. They could rarely take on considerable extra fuel and circle their destination awaiting an improvement as we were able to do. In 1953 a Comet broke up in a storm near Calcutta. There was an incident at the airport at Rome when a Comet failed to become airborne because the pilot had lifted the nose too high and too early on his take off run. Then in January 1954 a Comet en route from Rome to London fell out of the sky into the sea off Elba. Whilst a highly organised search for every part of the aircraft that could be recovered was in progress various modifications to the Comet were made in the hope that one or more of these would eliminate the unknown cause and after about ten weeks the aircraft was put back into service. Although there must have been a number who had misgivings the majority of Comet crews returned to flying still enthusiastic and undismayed, but in a few short weeks the disaster to another Comet which also plunged into the Mediterranean interrupted the jet age for a further four years. The Royal Navy was

The reconstruction at Farnborough of the Comet after the Royal Navy had salvaged parts from the Mediterranean.
*Royal Aircraft Establishment*

The fuselage of Comet G ALYU being tested to destruction in a specially built water tank at Farnborough.
*Royal Aircraft Establishment*

assigned the task of recovering every available scrap of the aircraft from the sea bed near Elba and each section was re-assembled at Farnborough. The hull of a new Comet was tested to destruction there and the point of fuselage failure was at last found. The De Havilland company and the Royal Aircraft Establishment published all their findings and the information was made readily available to Boeing and Douglas who at that time were several years behind Britain in the construction of a commercial jet aircraft.

Twenty-two Argonauts were then operating on B.O.A.C. routes and the type was no longer under construction. In any case the Argonaut was slower, noisier and carried fewer passengers than the Constellations which B.O.A.C. also operated. The Corporation scoured the world for spare Constellations and Stratocruisers to maintain our scheduled services. The Hermes had been so uneconomic to operate that most had already been sold or cocooned. The severe shortage of aircraft meant that some services had to be discontinued and the routes to South America were abandoned. The Bristol Britannias had already been ordered by the Chairman, Sir Miles Thomas, but it was to be another three years before they carried a paying passenger. First the development of the aircraft was seriously delayed by the destruction of the prototype in a forced landing and then the Proteus engines were plagued with "flame-out" whenever the aircraft entered cloud. Even so when Sir Miles Thomas left B.O.A.C. in 1956 the Corporation's financial results had been transformed from massive deficits to modest profits. Sir Miles was familiar to crews as he so frequently flew the routes. Of the half dozen or so chairmen during my time in B.O.A.C. he particularly earned the respect of the pilots for his keenness and enthusiasm in the face of enormous difficulties.

B.O.A.C. Chairman Sir Miles Thomas receives the log book of the first Bristol Britannia to be delivered to the airline.
*British Airways*

The year 1956 saw the loss of our first Argonaut. It took off from Kano in northern Nigeria during the rainy season and as it climbed through the first hundred feet ran straight into a thunderstorm "cell" developing invisibly in its path. It encountered a dramatic reversal of wind direction and losing all "lift" mushed back at full power into the ground where it caught fire and was destroyed. There were very few survivors among passengers and crew. I was in Tripoli at the time and operated the next service southbound to Kano whereupon I was delegated to lay a wreath at the mass burial of the victims. The funeral service had to be delayed several hours whilst carpenters worked frantically to construct sufficient coffins. The ceremony was attended by several members of the British Governor's staff formally attired in white uniforms and pith helmets. There were representatives too of the Emir of Kano, tall men, impressive in long robes. Among us in the official funeral party was a passenger who had survived the accident. Whilst he had suffered only minor injuries, his wife and child had died. Each of the Emir's men approached him in turn, bowing gravely. One by one they uttered the one word "condolences". When we finally arrived at the cemetery we found most of the European residents of Kano waiting quietly for the melancholy ceremony to begin. In due course an enquiry cleared both the captain and the airport controller of all responsibility for the accident. Neither the airport or the aircraft had radar to warn them of the developing thunderstorm "cell".

The crew on the flight deck of an Argonaut had been two pilots, a navigator and a radio officer but radio communications between ground and aircraft had been improved to the point where weather information and en route instructions by air trafffic control could be exchanged in clear speech without the need for transmissions in morse code. The radio officers had actually assisted in the elimination of their own jobs and final trials had been carried out with a radio officer travelling in the passenger cabin who was called upon for assistance by the pilots only as a last resort! Thus the crew members with their wavy gold braid received their handshake and departed whilst the pilots inherited their duties with the constant cacophony of sound and of course more money for the extra work. Some of the radio officers had obtained navigation licences and these remained with us for a few more years.

Most of the stewardesses who had joined the airline after leaving the military services had now left and younger girls who had been at school during the war were flying with us. An enquiry by a tactless pilot whether his new stewardess was an ex-Wren or Waaf brought the swift rejoinder that the war had long been over and that she had been about twelve years old on victory day. On the flight deck we were being joined by new pilots who had served in the R.A.F. or Fleet Air Arm in the post-war period on short service commissions or as national servicemen. Some of them had flown jet fighters such as Meteors or Venoms and on joining B.O.A.C. had to accustom themselves to flying slow piston-engined transports. All of us had to adapt ourselves to the very changed world in which we lived and worked. Nationalist pressures forced all large firms with world wide interests to engage fewer expatriates and more local staff. We watched with apprehension as Indians, Pakistanis and every other national cast off our engine cowlings and set about the duties which most of us had first seen done only by the more skilled R.A.F. tradesmen. As they had been carefully selected and trained by just such teachers we discovered with relief that the tasks were still being thoroughly done. In another sense too adjustments had to be made. Our former wartime enemies were now among our passengers, our customers and our clients. One pilot who regularly wrote on his passenger bulletin that the celebrated railway built by prisoners of war of the Japanese lay beneath the aircraft's track had tactfully to be persuaded to desist from so doing notwithstanding the fact that his brother had slaved and died there.

One innovation very welcome to crews was the introduction of meal allowances at stops down the routes. Previously there had been an all-in arrangement with hotels at which we were accommodated and it was not at all unusual for a crew which had flown all night to arrive at their hotel too late for breakfast. After sleeping through the middle of the day and missing lunch also it was very galling to have to wait for the dinner hour before the pangs of hunger could be assuaged. The meal allowances enabled the individual to eat wherever he liked at times to suit himself and if he slept through a normal mealtime at least he had saved himself some money. Other airlines already did this and sometimes we compared notes on the respective allowances. I remember the amusement of a Pan American pilot at our "tea allowance" and his willing agreement that it was an essential part of a civilised existence.

Another popular scheme to be introduced was staff holiday travel whereby for ten per cent of the ordinary return fare one could make journeys to places on the airlines' routes. A married man was permitted to take his wife and children and single staff their parents, but the privilege could only be exercised when seats remain unsold. There was always a period of anxious waiting until the final moment when the "ship's papers" were closed. Length of service, not company rank, decided the order of allocating seats. Sometimes it was necessary to disembark at a point along the route in favour of a fare-paying passenger but the scheme was well patronised and earned the airline additional revenue by filling seats which would otherwise have been empty.

There were occasions when aircraft were delayed by fog or a lack of spares, the "slipping" pattern became disrupted and crews returned home later than expected. It was

The author with his wife Pat and daughters Robin and Francesca travelling to Chile on holiday.

always difficult to notify one's family when this happened or to let them know the new itinerary when one was fortunate enough to know it oneself. There was no department responsible for informing the relatives of crew members and when the wife of an overdue pilot made a telephone call to the Operations office she might not succeed in obtaining any reliable information. The Operations officers were more concerned about the movement of aeroplanes than the crews who flew them. A wife who had been on her own for a number of days was naturally concerned when her husband failed to reappear. It made matters worse to be unable to discover how many hours or days were likely to pass before she could expect to see him again.

"What shall we tell this woman?" my wife overheard a harrassed clerk remark. On my return home I promised to try and remedy this situation but the senior member of the Argonaut fleet management to whom I spoke was unsympathetic. "You should not have joined if you wanted regular working hours," he told me. "It is inevitable that you will sometimes be delayed abroad. When a crew is likely to be more than seven days late we send a postcard to the men's homes to advise the family of this fact."

Our conversation was interrupted by a telephone call from the manager's wife. Evidently she wished to know what time to expect him that evening. When he had given her this information I felt I had made my point and left his office. In fact I had achieved nothing and several years passed before an information service for the families of crew members was instituted.

The wife of an airline pilot has to put up with a number of aggravations which can and sometimes do wreck marriages. She may accept that her husband will be abroad on her birthday, their wedding anniversary and Christmas Day. The grass may grow so long in his absence that a lawnmower which will not start may be only a minor inconvenience. But it can strain her equanimity to breaking point when a child develops whooping cough on a day that has seen her husband pack his bathing trunks, tennis kit and summer clothing for a two week foray to the Caribbean.

An unexpected call to report to the airport at very short notice frequently produces heated exchanges between indignant pilots and the clerks whose job it is to roster the crews. The clerks, both male and female have learnt to develop a tough outer shell. One resolute woman came to be known as Dracula's daughter.

"Dinger" received a summons to fly as a passenger on another airline to replace one of our pilots who had been taken ill in Canada. That evening patches of fog were spreading at London Airport and the aircraft captain was directed by the control tower from one runway to another and back again in an effort to comply with the required visibility limits. Almost an hour passed before the passengers felt the surge of power as the take-off run began but when a considerable speed had been built up the captain sensed that something was wrong and slammed the throttles into reverse power. But the DC8 sped off the end of the runway, ploughed across open country and finally came to rest in a cabbage field not far from the *Peggy Bedford Inn* on the Bath road.

Everyone scrambled out through the emergency exits as fast as they were able and "Dinger" pounded through the mud, fearful that the aircraft would explode before he had covered a safe distance. When he was out of danger his next thought was for his wife, how upset she would be if she first learned of the accident from a B.B.C. broadcast. Panting from his exertions, dishevelled, with mud up to his knees, he hurried into the company's crew office in the airport central area in search of a telephone. The clerk's face lit up in welcome. "Aha!" she said. "There you are, Mr Bell. Now if we waste no more time we can still get you to Canada tonight. There's another flight leaving at . . ."

Most of the pilots I know are rather good husbands and I am constantly put to shame by those who have themselves installed central heating or built on an extra bedroom in their free time between trips abroad. Of course there are some who play fast and loose with the girls while they are away and others who neglect their wives in favour of the golf course while they are at home. Our wives have had to be chauffeurs, gardeners and handymen on many occasions.

I am reminded of a captain who was being driven home after a long trip by his first officer who was a near neighbour. "I told the wife to paint the outside of the house while I was away," he remarked. "She should have been able to finish the job. By all accounts the weather has been fine and dry."

The first officer stopped the car by the gate of the captain's house and they both surveyed the property. Every door, window frame and lintel had been superbly primed and enamelled. "Not bad, not bad at all," the captain generously conceded and then his eyes fell upon the gate where they stood and he gave a sharp cry of dismay. "She's forgotten the damned gate! My God! One can't rely on a woman for any little thing."

Not all are such hard taskmasters. Many a stewardess having flown for a few years with the airline has married a pilot. She had certainly seen a broad spectrum of the flying species in that time and learnt how a pilot ticked. She must have discovered how much truth there was in the story that any conversation among pilots was about aeroplanes if it was not about sex, seniority or second-hand cars. Certainly it tended to exclude her. Nevertheless a large number of the girls have accepted the challenge and joined the brigade of wives who stay at home and wait.

British pilots are a conservative lot and hate what they suspect to be unnecessary change. They consider it entirely right and proper that English should be the accepted mode of communication between pilots and control centres on the ground, even if the conversation is between a Venezuelan pilot and a control tower operator in Brussels. For years we had used a phonetic alphabet which it was proposed to change for the benefit of foreigners. Thus a British aircraft call sign George Able Love How King became Gulf Alfa Lima Hotel Kilo. The new alphabet was accepted with great reluctance but having been learnt was quickly assimilated. Within a few years B.O.A.C. adopted the callsign of the flight number on which the aircraft was engaged instead of the registration letters. Since the war our prefix has been "Speedbird"; for Pan American it is "Clipper" and Aer Lingus is "Shamrock". Each airline has a derisory interpretation of a competitor's name. B.O.A.C. used to be called "Better on a camel" whilst T.W.A. is said to stand for "Teeny weeny airlines" or "Try walking across." Perhaps the most amusing translation is that suffered by the Belgian airline SABENA. "Such a bloody experience, never again."

# CHAPTER SEVEN

# Bristol Britannia. The Whispering Giant

IN 1956 Sir Gerald D'Erlanger succeeded Sir Miles Thomas as Chairman of B.O.A.C. All that summer the crisis that followed Colonel Nasser's nationalisation of the Suez Canal had been brewing up. The Britannias which had already been delivered to B.O.A.C. had not been put into passenger service because of problems with the engines but they were kept busy ferrying British troops to Cyprus. The crews who had regularly "slipped" at Cairo had witnessed the tension there. We had already moved from the city to a hotel in the residential suburb of Heliopolis, fairly near to the airport, to avoid incidents and demonstrations. As a further precaution the airline markings were painted out on the crew buses and a police guard with a sub-machine gun rode along with us to and from the airport. When the Anglo-French military intervention finally came there were fortunately no B.O.A.C. aircraft or crews in Cairo and our services to South and East Africa were re-routed through Libyan airports and to the Far East via Istanbul.

The long range version of the Britannia was urgently required to replace the Boeing Stratocruisers on the North Atlantic route. The latest Douglas airliner, the "Seven Seas" carried sufficient fuel to avoid calls at Gander or Goose Bay, Keflavik or Shannon. The DC7C could fly non-stop from London to New York or Toronto although the journey might take fourteen hours. It was not provided with bunks or a separate bar, amenities very popular with passengers on the slow and stately Stratocruisers as they had been a decade earlier on the flying boats. Sadly airline economies invariably result in the elimination of such benefits when there is an opportunity to fill space and sell more seats.

There had been an extra charge for a bunk which could be booked in advance or bought from the chief steward. The atmosphere in the aircraft bar was invariably convivial and it was not uncommon for a bunk to be occupied by two persons whose previous acquaintance was of no great duration. In the galley one night a call-bell rang at rhythmic intervals. "Bunk F" the stewardess noted and went to investigate. Pulling aside the curtain she observed a couple "in flagrante delicto" although the act was described to me less delicately as "on the job". The man's elbow was against the call button. "You're ringing the bell," his companion warned him. The man took this remark to be a compliment on his technique. "Baby," he replied, "you haven't felt anything yet."

The Britannia was finally introduced on the African routes in February 1957 but by then a long range version was also in production and I delayed my application for a posting until pilots for this fleet were required. I had been a long time on Argonauts and I particularly looked forward to flying a successful British aircraft across the North Atlantic where American aircraft manufacturers had so far enjoyed monopoly. Already we realised that the Britannia would reign supreme for only a short time. B.O.A.C. with the De Havilland Comet IV and Pan American with Boeing's 707 were both striving to be first to put a pure jet across the Atlantic. B.O.A.C. had also ordered the Boeing 707 to maintain its competitive position.

Each of B.O.A.C.'s various fleets had an identity of its own and the pilots were paid at different rates depending upon the type they flew. Those that flew on the North Atlantic were paid the most and for many years received a supplementary sum to compensate them for the exceptional rigours of the weather en route and at the necessary landing places. Many of B.O.A.C.'s most senior pilots, and naturally this included the remaining Imperial Airways men, were engaged upon the Atlantic route and many had flown it throughout the war on the air ferry service. The weather hazards were real and it must be remembered that before pressurised aircraft were available it was not usually possible to fly above the icing level and aircraft remained in cloud for hours at a time. These pilots had become accustomed to flying American aircraft during and immediately after the war. From Boeing flying boats they had gone on to Liberators, Constellations and Stratocruisers. With some justification they were scornful of British products such as the York, Hermes and Tudor.

Boeing Stratocruiser "Caledonia" in flight. *British Airways*

The rest of us had battled the Indian monsoons, African line squalls and sand storms and the inadequacies of the airports' facilities in many poverty stricken countries. To us the Atlantic "barons" as they had come to be called seemed to operate almost as a separate airline within B.O.A.C. A lot of this feeling was of course the sort of loyalty given to squadrons and regiments in the services. Those pilots on the Atlantic run who had flown American aircraft almost exclusively in their careers were wont to boast that they had never flown east of the Greenwich meridian. Yet the other routes certainly had their compensations. When it is winter in England it is winter in North America and a pretty fearsome one at that. Those who flew to Africa and to the East saw plenty of sunshine and usually had sufficient free time to acquire a suntan which addicts were able to keep throughout the year. A flying staff recreation club had been formed to which almost everyone contributed a few shillings a month and a sufficiently large fund was established to buy golf and tennis equipment and even a few sailing boats. These were positioned at stations where crews were "slipped" and for those less energetic "Scrabble" sets and playing cards were provided. Membership was arranged at local clubs. The benefits were enjoyed almost entirely by those on routes other than to North America partly because of the very high cost of club membership there and also due to the great distance of many clubs from the centre of the towns where the crews were lodged.

*　　*　　*　　*　　*　　*

In 1947 I had been handed the Lancastrian and York handbooks and having studied them in my own time taken a written examination to complete the two sets of answers in succession in little more than an hour. In 1950 there had been a three week intensive course on the Argonaut and the written examination occupied about two hours. The Britannia course in 1958 went on and on for at least six weeks and we were allowed three hours to sit the paper. The aircraft contained an enormous weight of electrical equipment and it taxed my limited technical knowledge to the utmost to master an adequate understanding of it all. Finally with the course behind us we drove down to Hurn airport for the far more enjoyable task of learning how to handle the new aircraft. The first pleasant surprise was to feel the enormous surge of power even on a top weight take off which carried the Britannia off the runway and into the air at a generous rate of climb. On Argonauts and other aircraft we had all known uncomfortable moments or even minutes when heavily laden out of some torrid place such as Khartoum it had seemed that the aircraft was never going to achieve its proper rate of climb.

After piston-engined aircraft the passenger cabin of the Britannia was pleasantly quiet but it earned the name "whispering giant" from the lack of any roar from the engines as it rose and climbed away from the runway. The pilots from the Argonaut flight who were assigned to fly it quickly became enthusiastic about its handling qualities. The cockpit was quite spacious and uncluttered by Aldis lamp, Very pistol and cartridges, all items which followed the collection of national flags into oblivion. Now at last we were provided with a storm warning radar screen. Obviously we could not always avoid flying into heavy cloud formations but the screen indicated the dangerous "cores" to avoid and every pilot must

A Britannia alongside the memorial to Alcock and Brown, London Airport.              *British Airways*

bless the inventor of this device. The range of the radar was over a hundred miles so even at the rapid speed of the Britannia there was ample time to choose a heading to achieve the smoothest ride. The radar screen also served to indicate coastlines, rivers, lakes and built-up areas. In place of the Eureka-Rebecca we had a D.M.E., a distance measuring device which indicated to the pilot on numeral counters the nautical miles separating the aircraft from the beacon which he had tuned. The maximum range of the D.M.E. was two hundred miles.

After so many days spent in a classroom and evenings at home devoted to extra study with fees to be paid if failure requires the examination papers to be written a second time, there is a special atmosphere of relief and enjoyment when one finds oneself "down the route" once more. When sufficient time is available between flights someone organises a party.

"Spud" and his crew celebrated in the room of a stewardess and by sunrise only he and she remained. "Your reputation will be ruined," said the gallant pilot "if I am seen to leave your room at this hour." Accordingly he knotted together the sheets, a blanket and the shower curtain, tied one end to the bedpost and departed in a far more precipitate fashion than he had intended through the window.

Seeing him silent and spreadeagled on the ground the alarmed stewardess summoned assistance over the telephone from another member of the crew whose imminent slumbers she had arrested in time. "You stay where you are," he advised, "we don't want a scandal. Leave it to me." His actions showed the best qualities of the diplomatic service. Aware that his stunned and prostrate colleague was a keen golfer known to enjoy an early round he scattered about his legs a golf bag and some clubs to give the impression that he had stumbled and fallen. Then he demanded help from the hotel staff.

In those days "Spud" had rather a dashing beard but it had disappeared when next we met. I expressed regret at the loss and asked the reason. "Well, it's like this," he explained, "a crew have a noisy room party and there are complaints. Inquiries are made to find anybody who was present to take the blame. Inevitably someone remembers a chap with a beard."

The British were soon to hand over the reins of government in many parts of the world where we travelled but occasionally one was confronted by relics of an earlier age. Approaching Nairobi the cabin staff had been handing out landing cards for disembarking passengers when the complexion of one elderly woman went brick-red and she demanded an audience with the captain. When I reached her side she remarked in regal tones "I will be residing at Government House. Surely I am not required to bother with this thing?"

I told her politely that she might be detained by the immigration authorities if she did not do so and left her bridling with indignation. That evening I was amused to read in the *East African Standard* that the Governor had temporarily left the colony.

It was pleasant to visit Kenya again and to enjoy the old-fashioned comforts of the *Norfolk Hotel*. In the men's washroom the admonition not to throw cigarette ends into the urinal still bore the carefully printed addition of the Governor's name but below this a visitor had neatly inscribed another notice. "No, they get wet, weedy and difficult to relight. Sir Gerald d'Erlanger."

To this day the *Norfolk Hotel* retains its old world charm, a pleasant contrast to the concrete palaces built to a pattern in every big city. Inevitably the Indian waiters have been replaced by Africans and there are guests of many other nationalities besides the British but it is noticeable that Kenyans and other black nationals prefer to patronise the new hotels. At a time when in the Western world dress for all times of the day has become extremely informal it is interesting to find the old rules zealously enforced by those now managing affairs in former colonies. In the *Norfolk* gentlemen are requested to wear jackets and ties in the evening and the African head waiter runs an eye over the attire of those who would enter his domain. A young American of my acquaintance was astonished to be refused admittance to the dining room when lunch was being served. In the United States imported Rugby shirts had enjoyed a vogue and he was wearing the colours of a famous London club. He pressed me for an explanation. "After all," he insisted, "that head waiter must have been taught discrimination by you British."

*    *    *    *    *    *

For many years pilots had practised instrument flying in the Link Trainer which contained only a pilot's seat opposite an instrument panel together with a throttle and control column. In 1957 this was replaced by a Britannia flight simulator which comprised a replica of the nose section of the aircraft and contained the entire flight deck area. Although simulators may cost a million pounds they save the airlines far greater sums which would be incurred in fuel costs and landing fees. Moreover instructors can safely demonstrate the correct actions to combat all manner of emergencies. Fires or double engine failures are hazardous if not impossible to simulate in the air.

Every year crew members go back to school to be reminded about the operation of the dinghies, the contents of the first aid kits, the use of dangerous drugs, the location of axes and fire extinguishers. We are shown films about ditching on the sea and emergency landings on or off airfields and have an opportunity to handle some of the safety equipment. When a mock-up cabin was constructed with the slide extended at the authentic angle to the ground an emergency evacuation became a routine practice drill. To spare the stewardesses any embarrassment overalls were offered to them. The first girl who pointed out the lack of logic in this chivalrous suggestion and projected herself boldly on to the slide suffered grievously for her spirit. The friction effect of nylon panties on the rubber slide severely scalded the poor girl's bottom.

In 1958 the Britannia went into service on the North Atlantic and in the same year a new route was established across the mid Atlantic to Venezuela and Colombia with stops at Bermuda, Antigua, Barbados and Trinidad. Caracas and Bogota had not previously seen a B.O.A.C. aircraft. The airport at Caracas is near the shore line with mountains towering to the north of the runway. The wind direction is usually from the east and a very careful final approach has to be made at an angle to the runway over the foothills of the mountains and the aircraft lined up just before crossing the threshold of the runway. It is almost as spectacular an arrival as that at Hong Kong and passengers sitting by the right hand side windows are quite startled at the sight of solid outcrops of rock so close to the wingtip. Bogota is a very high level airfield at over eight thousand feet and aircraft usually land towards the south east. At this airport aircraft taking off or making an overshoot must alter course to the south without delay to avoid mountain peaks up to twelve thousand feet beyond the runway's path.

The spacious cabin of the Britannia was much appreciated by the passengers and bunks were available at an extra charge as on the Stratocruisers. No longer was it necessary to offer cotton wool to passengers to deaden the noise of the engines. On some piston-engined aircraft on night flights passengers had become accustomed to the sight of sparks driven back from the exhaust tubes. On the Britannia there were occasional columns of flame to be seen as the igniters put sparks into the combustion chambers. This had proved to be the solution to the engine icing problem when the aircraft had been flying in cloud. It was rather a disconcerting sight when observed for the first time. The Britannia did not have the range to make every westbound crossing non-stop and Gander, Goose Bay and other bolt holes still saw a B.O.A.C. aircraft on occasions. Even so it was a delightful experience to fly the fastest and most comfortable aircraft and one which was also British on the North Atlantic.

The approach to Bogota airport, Colombia, 8355 feet above sea level.

Aerial view of the airport at Hong Kong.

The westbound crossing took about eleven hours and eastbound nine or ten hours. The majority of the Atlantic flights departed late in the evening from both London and New York and often included scheduled stops at Manchester, Prestwick and Boston. The time spent on duty was so long that a couple of crew bunks were installed aft of the flight deck and the pilots and flight engineer took turns to snatch a couple of hours rest on the crossing. In the winter the captain's ability to obtain any sleep was often inhibited by the weather broadcasts reporting deteriorating conditions at the destination and alternate airports.

It was very difficult to heat the cockpit area adequately at very high altitudes and a lot of blankets were required to keep oneself warm in the bunk. To our dismay an extra row of three passenger seats was installed across the aisle from the crew bunks. We found it most disconcerting to tumble from a bunk and have to tuck in our shirts and adjust our dress in front of those seated there. Many passengers wish to envisage the pilot as a man permanently at the controls and maintaining a watchful vigil. Shocked dismay was often evident upon their faces when the dishevelled and unshaven commander emerged blearily from behind the curtained area of the bunks.

To fix his position over the Atlantic ocean the navigating officer depended primarily on a system called Loran. Master and Slave stations on land transmitted pulses which the navigator interpreted from a cathode ray tube. He then referred to his chart which was over-printed with Loran chain lines. Useful assistance was also obtained from the Ocean Station Vessels whose positions were also marked on the charts. The principal function of these ships is to report sea and weather conditions but they have a fine record for assistance to shipping and in 1947 one of them rescued all on board a flying boat which ran out of fuel, and alighted on the ocean. Most of the vessels are manned by the Americans but Britain, Canada and France each muster one ship. All are equipped with radar screens and provided the aircraft navigator can pass a reasonably accurate estimate of his position the ship's radar operator can identify the aircraft and declare its bearing and distance from the ship. The men on the American ships are always delighted to talk to aircraft and sometimes ask for short messages to be telephoned or posted to their relatives ashore. The British ship is more formal and in my experience requests to the French for a radar fix invariably bring the reply that they are too busy sending up a radiosonde balloon or that the radar is temporarily unserviceable.

Britannia captains without previous experience of the American routes were required to make several flights under supervision. The reason was the intense pressure of air traffic at such busy centres as New York and Chicago. The flow of aircraft into and out of Chicago's O'Hare airport with two or three runways in use at the same time has always depended on immediate understanding and compliance with the controller's orders and these could sometimes be perplexing to a pilot not conversant with some of the local jargon. For example O'Hare airport is colloquially known as "the orchard" and may be referred to as such. The stream of aircraft approaching and touching down is timed meticulously so that the last to land is just clearing the runway as its successor crosses the threshold at about fifty feet. The sight would appal the calm unhurried controllers at London Airport who keep landing aircraft at least two miles apart.

It was also necessary to learn some new expressions. Approaching New York one day I failed to obtain all three green lights to indicate that my undercarriage was locked down. I warned the control tower of my difficulty and said that I would "overshoot" if unable to clear the snag in time for the landing. The trouble, a failed bulb, was remedied in time but as I touched down I was surprised to find fire engines, a foam tender and other vehicles racing alongside the runway. Evidently they had expected me to roll off the end. Their word for "overshoot" is to "pull up". A take-off which we "abandon" they "abort" and there are other different expressions.

If Chicago was a strain on one's concentration and understanding New York's Idlewild (later renamed Kennedy) presented the puzzle of which runway one would be likely to use. Invariably one was cleared to make an approach on the single runway equipped for an instrument approach and then at about seven hundred feet as one descended through the clouds the control tower would instruct the pilot to turn this way or that and make his way round to a totally different runway. The wind direction was often no clue. The proximity of La Guardia airport and the strength of protest from communities being overflown by noisily descending aircraft had relegated such basic wisdoms to second or third place.

In addition to flying across the Atlantic to cities in Canada and the United States the Britannia also flew from points in North America to the West Indies. It seemed extraordinary to take off from the extreme rigours of a Canadian winter with the prospect of landing in blazing sunshine a few hours later. Often the aircraft had first to be sprayed with de-icing fluid and then as we taxied out to the runway great care had to be taken to prevent the outboard propellers from striking the piles of snow banked along the taxiways. The ability to reverse the propellers on landing for the purpose of deceleration was of doubtful value when the result was the production of a blinding snowstorm before one. Sometimes we flew white-faced Canadians, eyes puffy from their gross central heating, south to the Caribbean sunshine and within the hour we were northbound again, their mahogany or lobster coloured compatriots on board, incongruous in straw hats and Bermuda shorts.

Every traveller has his own choice story of the horrors of air travel but one horror which all fear is to become separated from their luggage. With the best organisation and the best will in the world the human element is always present in the labelling directions and handling of baggage. This hazard even finds crew members and other company staff as well as the ordinary passenger among its victims. Occasionally quite remarkable oversights occur.

One day I was required to fly a Britannia from London to Venice, the aircraft having been chartered by a very eminent group, from the City of London liveried guilds. All on board had been promised absolutely first class service and prior to our departure I agreed to a request by the chief steward that the crew would have a late lunch on our arrival at Venice so that the cabin staff could give their entire attention to the passengers. We delivered them safely and on time and limousines whisked them away to their hotel with no tiresome formalities such as the Customs inspection, so important were this group. My crew enjoyed an excellent late lunch in the airport restaurant and returned to the aircraft to fly it empty back to London.

As I walked down the steps to the crew bus parked alongside the aircraft at London Airport the driver drew my attention to the rear hold which the ground staff had just opened. It was packed tight with expensive looking suitcases. Quite appalled I warned the traffic department of the oversight and as I drove home I imagined the various repercussions. The passengers whose baggage had not arrived at the hotel would have telephoned to the airport. At first they would have been told that it was on its way. When the full realisation of their personal disaster was apparent there would no doubt have been telephone calls to London Airport, both by B.E.A. who had handled us at Venice and by a spokesman for the passengers. He would probably have demanded to speak to the chairman of B.O.A.C.

The baggage had been left on board because the local staff at Venice, unfamiliar with the Britannia which did not normally call there, had overlooked the existence of the separate holds. If they had studied the load sheet with which they were equally unfamiliar they would have realised their error but they failed to do so. The captain is responsible for the aircraft and signs the load sheet prior to each flight. Usually he makes sure that the trim is correct and that the correct amount of fuel is on board. He takes it for granted that the weight and distribution in the various holds is as stated. No flight would ever leave on time if he queried it and checked each item. The missing baggage was flown out as quickly as possible on a Viscount. Later both corporations had to decide which should bear the cost of the extra flight.

# CHAPTER EIGHT

# The VC10. A Pilot's Aeroplane

THE predominance of the Britannia as the fastest, quietest airliner operating across the Atlantic was to be short-lived. In December 1958 the Comet at long last reappeared in the skies as the Mark IV and made the inaugural jet service to New York. A few weeks later Pan American Airways followed with the first Boeing 707. The delays that had dogged the introduction of the Britannia and the early disasters to the Comet had whittled away the sales potential of these two types. The Comet IV had to make a refuelling stop on most westbound crossings and was replaced by B.O.A.C.'s own Boeing 707s when these were delivered. It was some consolation for the British aircraft industry that the Boeing 707 and another competitor, the Douglas DC8, were offered to airlines with Rolls-Royce engines and a number of companies had made this choice in preference to an American engine.

Whilst the Britannias, Comets and our own Boeings were being delivered the old Argonauts and the stop-gap "Seven Seas" were being phased out but it was 1960 before the last services were flown and the Argonauts found ready buyers among overseas airlines and charter companies. The Britannias flew their slower schedules across the Atlantic at a lower fare than the jets, this being called the "propeller differential", but it was clear that the lower fare would not be permitted for long as one airline after another obtained jet equipment. Work had to be found for the Britannias and increasingly I found myself engaged on flights with groups who had chartered the aircraft for round trips to Europe from Boston, Philadelphia, Syracuse, Toronto and other cities. On two occasions I flew to Buenos Aires, once with a British Army band and on another occasion to pick up the crew of an oil tanker.

There were also flights to bring a full complement of West Indians to Britain ahead of the legislation then being introduced to prevent such wholesale immigration. The obvious en-route refuelling point was Bermuda but because of the difficulty anticipated in accommodating these passengers in luxury hotels in the event of an overnight delay the flights were routed via New York. I carried immigrants on several flights to Britain. They always travelled in their best clothes and were very quiet and subdued. Tired after their long flight they would often ask how they could travel on to such towns as Manchester or Nottingham and many of them were duped by heartless taxi drivers who took their money and left them in Slough or Hounslow.

One new piece of equipment to be fitted on all our aircraft was a public address system whereby either the pilot or a member of the cabin staff could address the passengers. Everyone who has travelled by air will have their own opinion about the use or misuse of this instrument. Sometimes it is inaudible or indistinct and whilst some captains use it sparingly others bombard their unfortunate passengers with reports that the aircraft is passing over places which only a small proportion of those on board can see from their seats, assuming that they wish to do so. A colleague who was over-indulgent in this practice found the chief steward at his side brandishing a ten dollar bill. "Gentleman in seat 3B sends this, sir," he confided, "and there will be another one for you on arrival in New York if he doesn't hear another word from you."

One story, possibly apocryphal, concerns an Australian pilot who spoke some concluding words to his passengers as they approached their destination and then, unaware that he was still pressing the "transmit" button, remarked to his co-pilot: "What I need now is a cold beer and a hot woman." To prevent any further disclosures the stewardess rushed forward towards the cockpit and a passenger called after her; "Don't forget his cold beer."

It became the practice to use the public address system before each flight to describe to passengers the emergency equipment and simultaneously the stewardesses demonstrate how to put on the lifejackets. Formerly one of the cabin attendants had to explain all this over the roar of the engines starting up. There was one old steward who particularly resented those passengers who remained hidden behind newspapers and paid no attention. "You, sir," he would call, "yes, you in seat 4A. This is for your benefit, not for mine. I know it all. I would thank you to pay attention." And they did.

The cabin crew had served breakfast to a full complement of passengers when I heard this announcement. "Kindly remain seated until we have been able to recover all your trays. Afterwards by all means leave your seats but please don't all go back to the toilets at the rear of the aircraft . . . the tail goes down . . . the nose comes up . . . the captain gets furious . . . and I will get the blame."

For many years some airlines had issued certificates to the passengers when they were borne across the Equator. Someone had to enter each person's name, the date, flight number and the meridian of longitude on a document which proclaimed the usual gibberish familiar to anyone who has crossed the Equator in a cruise ship. This unwelcome chore usually fell upon the navigator. When the number of passengers on each aircraft increased B.O.A.C. abolished the certificates and substituted "Junior jet log books" which together with a badge are presented to children. At the beginning and end of each school term they travel in large groups and we are not always very polite when a stewardess arrives at our side with an enormous stack of these books. Each sector of the flight has a column allotted for the captain to sign.

*　　*　　*　　*　　*　　*

In one's working life it is odd incidents and the unexpected meeting with an old colleague that reminds one of the passage of time. I was in a fish queue one Friday in the neighbourhood of my house with my shopping instructions on a piece of paper and bag in hand. Immediately in front was a young woman with two small children. As she received her order and paid the fishmonger she turned and gave a start of recognition. "Oh! You are Captain Jackson. I did my very first trip with you as a stewardess in B.O.A.C. . . ."

I looked nervously at the fishmonger and sensed the long queue waiting perhaps less patiently to be served, but a long reminiscence was in progress. "Two days in Rome and we all went to the beach. I got terribly burned and could hardly sit down but Tim had some camomile and was terribly kind." The fishmonger and the queue were spellbound and hanging on every word. All thoughts of plaice fillets and cods roes were banished from their minds. "Do you remember?" she ended at last.

I looked at the children and lamely apologised. "It must have been some time ago." "Only six years," she replied.

Certainly stewardesses arrived and departed in rapid succession but most of the pilots went on, gradually getting older and whilst I was on Britannias the last of the former Imperial Airways pilots were leaving B.O.A.C., Captains Jones, Messenger, Buxton and Percy amongst them. Few pilots were being released from the Royal Air Force and new pilots were being chosen by B.O.A.C. and B.E.A. and trained at the college at Hamble where the course lasted about eighteen months. Those who came to B.O.A.C. were "converted" to the aircraft which they were to fly and given further navigational instruction to obtain the necessary licences. They flew with us as second officers. Over the years a considerable proportion of the pilots had obtained navigation licences and those non-pilot navigators of wartime vintage who had themselves taught and supervised the practical navigation of the pilots were declared redundant. A few had obtained pilot's licences but most left and many found employment with other airlines at home and abroad.

One day a Lufthansa pilot on the ground at Kennedy airport requested in guttural tones a "clearance" for Frankfurt. The New York controllers are busy men who waste no time over words and are apt to forget that other nations speak other tongues. The speed of the clearance delivered with a strong Bronx accent evidently defeated the German, for a moment later the clearance was requested again by a very English voice. Once more it was delivered and this time it was repeated back without difficulty and acknowledged. A short silence was broken by another very English voice. "What's it like?" it asked, "working for the Krauts."

I was flying to New York on one occasion from Manchester and as London and most of the European continent was totally fogbound the Boston area controller was very much less busy than usual. A woman pilot of a light aeroplane from Poughkeepsie to Martha's Vineyard reported her position and gave her callsign, Alfa Mike. The controller was in a playful mood. "You are doing a great job ma'am," he said "and I re-assign you the callsign Able Mabel." From time to time she called up to report her position and entering into the spirit of things used this new call sign. After a while an American airline pilot who had entered the area became curious and asked what this Able Mabel was about. He received a cheerful explanation and a short silence ensued. Then, "I thought it was a guy with a tight seatbelt," he replied. "I was sure worried."

Superfluous conversation is discouraged in the busy skies above Britain but I remember occasions when humour was unconsciously supplied and again by Americans. Like foreign currency, standardisation of necessary information is regrettably absent from the aviation scene. Thus one must be careful to ascertain whether visibility is expressed in miles or kilometres, cloud base in feet or metres, temperature in centigrade or fahrenheit. In the United States an altimeter setting is given in inches of mercury and in Britain it is expressed in millibars. I heard the pilot of an American military flight ask a British airport for an altimeter setting. "One zero one three" he was told and utterly nonplussed he asked for it to be repeated. After a few moments of complete silence another American voice was heard, clear and to the point. "Don't touch it, Al, that's horse shit."

*　　*　　*　　*　　*　　*

When Sir Gerald d'Erlanger gave up the chairmanship of B.O.A.C. in 1960 the aircraft fleets in service were the Boeing 707, the Comet IV and the Britannias. The piston-engined types had all been displaced. Before he left he ordered about forty Vickers VC10s. In later years there was controversy over this number but it is known that Vickers demanded a sufficiently large order for production to be worth while. The aircraft was designed to enable a substantial payload to be carried out of airfields in tropical climates

Boeing 707 seen against a wintry landscape.　　　　　　　　　　　　　　*British Airways*

B.O.A.C. Chairman Sir Matthew Slattery.  *British Airways*

with limited runway lengths and situated at high levels. Nairobi and Johannesburg were two examples.

The new chairman was Sir Matthew Slattery who was to remain until 1963. The managing director was Sir Basil Smallpiece who had already been in B.O.A.C. for some time. In the course of a few years a large number of piston-engined aircraft had been offered for sale for whatever they would fetch and expensive new machines had to be paid for. Although there were a number of airports with short runways which a Comet but not a Boeing could use, the list was getting shorter and the Comets which could carry fewer passengers were becoming uncompetitive. The Britannias with their three tons of electrical equipment were very expensive to maintain and operate. Against the increasing number of jets they were even less able to compete and gradually became relegated to charter work.

Severe financial losses were being suffered which, together with the corporation's old debts, led Sir Matthew to describe B.O.A.C.'s financial structure as "bloody crazy". The British government set up a committee which looked into B.O.A.C.'s affairs and the subsequent Corbett report, which was never made public, was evidently very critical of the corporation's management. The Minister of Aviation asked for the resignation of the board of B.O.A.C. He appointed as chairman Sir Giles Guthrie.

Whilst all this was going on the VC10 was in production and courses for converting pilots and engineers were in progress. I had declined the opportunity to go to the Boeing a year or two earlier because I wanted once again to fly a British aircraft and one which I hoped would turn out to be a winner. The VC10 was late being delivered to B.O.A.C. but the time could be measured in months rather than in years. Its fuel consumption was found to be a little higher than the Boeing driven by similar Rolls-Royce engines. This was due to the extra drag incurred by the aircraft's massive T-tail. Also it had a slightly shorter range than the Boeing. On the other hand it was ideally suited for the task for which it was designed. No other jet could lift a full load of passengers and freight from Nairobi and carry them non-stop to Frankfurt or London, a distance of over 3,000 miles.

It is always a pleasure to complete the initial ground school course with its tests and examinations on each separate part of the aircraft, the burning of midnight oil. With that behind us we went to Shannon Airport in Ireland for flying instruction. Shannon is used for airline training because the landing charges compare favourably with those at British airports. There is little commercial traffic and very few people reside close enough to suffer the noise of aircraft constantly landing and taking-off.

We were impressed at once by the appearance of the VC10 and the expression, a "pilot's aeroplane" was often heard. When one sits for the first time in the pilot's seat the full significance of the term "swept-back wings" is apparent. It is only just possible to see the wingtips by pressing one's face against the cockpit windows. The handling characteris-

Built by Vickers at Weybridge, the Super VC10.  *British Airways*

tics of the aircraft met our full approval as normal landings were followed by practice with one or two engines throttled back to simulate power failures.

Familiar to former Comet pilots but new to those of us from Britannias were the speedbrakes on the upper surface of the wings. When it is necessary to achieve a very rapid rate of descent, perhaps because the controller has withheld permission due to other traffic, the pilot can pull back a lever which raises the speedbrakes, effectively eliminating the "lift" provided by the airflow over the wing surface.

Those whose business it is to quote insurance rates for commercial aircraft expect a few accidents to occur before the differing handling characteristics of a new type are generally understood by the operators. The jet-propelled airliner was no exception to this rule. Pilots of unpressurised aircraft had descended at about 300 feet a minute to spare the passengers discomfort to their ears. When cabins were pressurised pilots descended more rapidly but the ability to lose altitude at 5,000 feet a minute is a trap for the unwary. During descent jet engines are idling and take five seconds or more to develop full power, a longer time to arrest a larger rate of descent. In the United States at this time a great many crews were converting from conventional propeller driven aircraft to the Boeing 727 and a series of accidents to this type were attributed to the failure of the pilots to recognise this potential hazard.

At the altitude commonly flown by the jets the airspeed indicator's inaccuracy has displaced its use in favour of the machmeter and many airliners cruise at a mach number of 0.82 or 82 per cent of the speed of sound. It is the flight engineer's duty during the cruise to maintain the correct number by judicial use of his own set of throttles. If the aircraft exceeds this speed by only a small margin the blare of a warning horn alerts the crew and the pilots may demand a beer at the engineer's expense for his lack of attention. He gets his own back if the pilots allow the airspeed to fall too low on the approach, before the undercarriage has been lowered. Then the horn again blares its warning.

The VC10 also has an altimeter with a direct read-out of numerals like the miles run counter of a car. This has eliminated errors made by pilots misreading the old type of altimeter with three separate pointers tor tens, hundreds and thousands of feet. Several disasters are on record due to aircraft mistakenly being flown 10,000 feet below the intended altitude.

On this aircraft I first used the "Doppler" device which presents the crew with a continuous indication of drift and ground speed. This information is particularly valuable because at the levels flown by modern aircraft winds of over 100 knots are often encountered and the accompanying drift can easily carry one well off the intended track before a "fix" reveals the shift in windspeed and direction.

Another device, the transponder, enables radar controllers on the ground to identify the aircraft. Presented with a huge number of targets he has only to ask the pilot to "squawk ident" and we press a button which increases the size of our blip on his radar screen.

The VC10 is the only aircraft I have flown which contains a lavatory within the cockpit area, specifically for crew use. No longer has it been necessary to switch on the "fasten seatbelt" sign to expel an occupant and gain instant access.

Before the VC10 entered service it became known that the new chairman was trying to cancel orders for a substantial number of the aircraft, possibly the whole lot. This posed a dilemma for the minister, Julian Amery. He had held the former management to blame for the huge deficit which B.O.A.C. had incurred and promised the new board that the airline would be compensated if it was compelled by government directive to act contrary to its own commercial judgement.

Like other nationalised industries B.O.A.C. employed too many men but the proliferation of aircraft types, each requiring a back-up of spares along the airline routes had also contributed to the high cost of operations. Guthrie believed that it would make better economic sense to buy more Boeings. Eventually the usual British compromise was worked out and only seven of the aircraft on order were cancelled, but the controversy with its attendant publicity ruined the prospect of sales to other operators.

When sufficient aircraft were delivered to commence services the passenger response was extremely enthusiastic but from all sides came the question: "What is wrong with this aircraft? Why don't B.O.A.C. like it?" Among ourselves the argument also raged. On one side those of us who believed it to be a splendid machine, on the other pilots who had flown a succession of American aircraft, the "Boeing lobby" as they are sometimes called. Their sympathies were all with Sir Giles Guthrie.

The new chairman pruned the numbers of both ground and flying staff, inviting those who had served longest to retire early with the inducement of a "golden handshake". He also decided to sell B.O.A.C.'s country residence at Sunningdale. For many years the function of this comfortable and rather charming old house had been to accommodate crew members required for flights departing in the early hours of the morning or others who landed late at night.

The accommodation of airline crews throughout the world must inevitably rank as an enormous charge to the operator. As cabin staff numbers grow larger the cost is rising and it will not have escaped the notice of many travellers that airlines always put their crews in high quality hotels. The reason is not hard to find. The crews often arrive or depart in the middle of the night. Therefore the hotel must have a night staff to clean the rooms and to change the linen and towels ready for the next crew arriving to occupy those same beds. A telephone in each room is essential in order that the occupants can be wakened at any time or perhaps warned that the flight is late and the pick-up an hour or more later than planned. Modest establishments would be unable to cope with this sort of problem. Many hotels offer the airlines a favourable contract rate for the block booking of rooms throughout the year. Some hotels are very empty indeed in the "off-season".

In the past B.O.A.C. has owned its own accommodation. There was a guesthouse in Karachi with a swimming pool and tennis court. A similar place in Santiago had existed before the South American route to Chile was abandoned and changing slip crew patterns left the Khartoum guesthouse unnecessary. The abandonment of flying boat services ended the need for the houseboat at Rod-el-farag on the Nile which had served as accommodation for the crew at Cairo. One resthouse remembered with no affection at all by long serving

B.O.A.C. crews was at Dakar in West Africa. It had no sooner opened than a bus terminal was established nearby and sleep was also interrupted by an open air cinema and mosque in adjoining streets. A cock which crowed too early and too often in the yard of the adjoining building was murdered by one desperate sleeper. It is unlikely that accommodation exclusively for crews will be provided in the future but the airline has itself become part owner of hotels in places lacking sufficient accommodation for the increasing number of air travellers and visitors.

*  *  *  *  *  *

During the whole period of my flying service with B.S.A.A. and then B.O.A.C. I had been living in South Buckinghamshire, an easy half hour's drive to London Airport. For various reasons my wife and I had decided to move further west and the interval between the completion of my VC10 conversion course and the commencement of services in April 1964 seemed a good opportunity to look around for a new house and to make a move. We were greatly attracted to an old house in a small Oxfordshire village. It was built in Cotswold stone and the garden was similarly walled. Unfortunately our first good impression was ruined by the dreadful explosion of noise as an American Air Force 707 tanker rose sulphurously from the air base at nearby Brize Norton. We decided to think again but nothing else that we saw seemed as attractive. Eventually we decided to revisit the village and ask local people, the parson, schoolteacher and the old lady in the next door cottage, whether the noise level was tolerable. All of them insisted that they were not bothered and that in any case the Americans were leaving Brize Norton in a few months time. Not entirely convinced we went to an inn a few miles away directly under the flight path to the runway. Here I subjected the landlord to a careful inquisition before going to the washroom prior to taking lunch. When I returned to the bar I found him roaring with laughter. Apparently he had turned to my wife after my departure and asked her if I had some neurosis about aeroplanes or whether I was of an extremely nervous disposition.

Eventually we bought the house and soon afterwards the Americans departed. There was a blessed year of peaceful silence before the R.A.F. arrived in force with Belfasts and their own squadron of VC10s. The officers' mess graciously made me an honorary member and their number was at first so small that I came to know many of them very well including their air traffic controllers. The airway known as Upper Green One passes south of Brize Norton and I would sometimes give them a call when returning to London Airport from New York. Often they would telephone my wife to tell her that I would shortly be on my way home. The R.A.F. station has become more busy and the noise of the jets grows no less. I have a suspicion that long after I have ceased flying there will still be a VC10 at the bottom of my garden.

The Britannia has the quietest engines of any airliner ever built, astonishing those in close proximity as it takes off. However soundproof the VC10 is to those sitting within it the same cannot be said by those below its path as it becomes airborne and climbs away. Consequently all of us were required to learn the "noise abatement" drill applicable to jets. This remains in force at many airports around the world, particularly those situated close to towns and cities. Zurich bans all night departures within certain hours and London Airport also imposes restrictions. A typical drill is to reduce power ninety seconds after the start of the take-off run until a certain altitude is reached. Although accepted by pilots the practice is generally unpopular. At high weights pilots prefer to have all the power they can obtain from their engines and at times the power reduction is required when the aircraft is banking on to its first course from the airport. It is not unusual for the aircraft actually to descend until power is restored: but to those of us new to jets the sudden reduction in power was often most startling on a low weight take-off when the aircraft had been climbing steeply. The nose had to be lowered very smartly indeed to compensate for the sudden loss of indicated air speed on the dial. Nevertheless the public demand for less noise is justified and pilots exert every effort to comply. Listening posts around many airports monitor every take-off and measure the decibel count. A reading over the permitted level results in a complaint to the airline who in turn require an explanation from the captain.

We had a simulator for the VC10 and a second one was delivered with a visual display of a runway which could be revealed to the pilot at whatever altitude the instructor wished. This was achieved by linking the manoeuvres of the simulator to a television camera directed at a model airport in a country setting. An instrument approach could thus be concluded by an apparent descent through a very low cloud base and a "visual" landing performed. Another development was the showing of films of airports to pilots for familiarisation purposes. B.O.A.C. and a few other airlines made the films using a light aeroplane and copies could be bought by other companies to show to their own pilots.

This was a great advance on the expensive and wasteful system of sending one captain to supervise another into an airfield several thousand miles away. A film shows the approach to each runway in perfect weather. The "personal visit" had often been made at night and in such poor weather that the runway lights were all that one saw. In such conditions one runway looks much like another. Airports with exceptional local features like Hong Kong with its surrounding mountains still merit a special journey and so does New York but only for the complexity of its air traffic control. One result of the introduction of airport familiarisation films was the abandonment of the restriction of pilots to a limited number of routes and most of us welcomed the opportunity to fly the whole range of routes served by the particular aircraft we flew.

I was to discover very early how carefully one needed to watch the fuel consumption of a jet. I had left London on a flight to Kuwait with stops at Amman and Baghdad. Arriving over Amman after sunset I was instructed to hold and await approach clearance. After ten minutes it transpired that the runway lights were switched off and no one in the tower knew how to light them. I had sufficient fuel to fly on to Baghdad where the weather had been forecast as good and wasted no further time but continued on my way. Before long I was considerably alarmed to receive a new weather report that visibility at Baghdad was reduced by rising sand whipped up by strong winds. I arrived overhead before conditions became really serious but my landing was further delayed by other aircraft which had also diverted. A combination of circumstances such as these can never be predicted but give the pilot a few more grey hairs.

# CHAPTER NINE

# The Jets Spread Their Wings

THE VC10 had entered service in April 1964, initially to West Africa and subsequently to East and South Africa. Like all newly introduced aircraft it had its teething troubles but none that were not overcome before long. The air conditioning was troublesome at first and the flaps had their design snags. The landing lights did not always extend when required. On one occasion I circled Kano in northern Nigeria trying to lock down the undercarriage preparatory to a landing. The port side main wheels would not extend despite frequent up and down selections of the undercarriage lever. When the emergency "free fall" drill was used the port wheels extended and the last resort of "winching" produced the desired green light on our instrument panel.

Once on the ground the engineers raised the aircraft on jacks and I watched as they first retracted the undercarriage then selected the lever down once more. Three or more times the cycle was successfully achieved but then the defect was reproduced and the port wheels remained in their housing although some fearsome knocking noises could be heard. As the engineers conferred a seasonal line squall appeared on the horizon menacing us with its black rolls of lower and upper cloud, sharp stabs of lightning and reverberating thunder. It became imperative to lock the undercarriage down and lower the aircraft from the jacks because the approaching squall might topple it. As the wind forces increased the engineers anxiously worked and succeeded in locking down the wheels. Minutes later the squall line crossed the airfield.

Signals were exchanged with London and before long I was instructed to fly the aircraft back to England in ballast with the undercarriage to be left extended. Obviously this would restrict our speed and height and the drag would increase the fuel consumption. I was very suspicious of the optimistic fuel consumption figure signalled to me to be used for planning the flight and ordered the tanks to be filled to capacity. During the climb it was soon apparent that we were using over twelve thousand kilograms of fuel an hour and on levelling out at the maximum ceiling I could achieve, twenty-five thousand feet, the consumption was about ten thousand kilograms an hour which is three thousand gallons. It was clear that I could not hope to reach London and even Rome was out of range so I altered course for Madrid and landed there. When we had refuelled and reached London we were aware that we were providing a set of fuel consumption figures for flight with the undercarriage extended that had previously been totally lacking.

One did not carry passengers under such conditions, or when a VC10 was found to require an engine change before carrying passengers upon the next stage of their journey, but the VC10 could be ferried with one engine inoperative in ballast from one airfield to

Reflected in the rain covered tarmac a VC10 outside the B.O.A.C. hangar at London Airport. *British Airways*

another where a spare engine was available. Sometimes quite long distances were involved and I once flew from Los Angeles to New York having first made sure that a number of possible landing places en route had acceptable weather conditions. The rear mounted engines made handling no problem to the VC10 pilot. A three engine ferry was not an exercise available to those flying the Boeing 707, but both types of aircraft sometimes flew with a "fifth pod", an engine slung under the wing.

In this manner engines could be moved and positioned about the routes. The extra"pod" made no noticeable difference in handling and the effect of the increased drag on fuel consumption was minimal.

I had looked forward to flying the VC10 to South America when the Comet was replaced but sadly B.O.A.C. abandoned that route for the second time, convinced that it

The four Rolls-Royce Conway engines below the VC10 tail.                    *British Airways*

was unprofitable. British United Airways had also acquired VC10s. They applied for and obtained permission to replace B.O.A.C.'s services and were operating these within a few weeks of our last Comet services to that continent. The reasons for the lack of profit on the South American route were the low number of services to numerous stations each with resident B.O.A.C. staff, together with restrictions imposed by the republics on the numbers of seats allowed to be sold between the various points. B.U.A. offered no extra frequencies but cut costs by using local agencies for handling their services. They too found themselves hard pressed to make any profits on the route.

When all twelve standard VC10s had been delivered the stretched version, the Super VC10 followed. This carried more passengers and the range was improved by finding space for almost fifteen hundred gallons of extra fuel in the huge fin beneath the massive T-tail structure. As these aircraft were delivered so were our routes extended and in April 1965 the Super VC10 was heralded by the advertisers as the "new shape in the Atlantic skies". Always eager to try a new product the American and Canadian passengers appreciated the smooth ride and quieter cabin. We would often cruise a little faster than the Boeing and Douglas jets and point out to our passengers our competitors at higher or lower levels whom we were overtaking.

This did not always happen. On one occasion after I had overtaken a T.W.A. Boeing as both of us approached the holding stack for Kennedy airport my announcement to the passengers coincided with an urgent request by the T.W.A. captain to the controller. "I have a stork on my wingtip," he radioed "Get me down—but fast!" Suspiciously we watched him sweep past us and descend rapidly towards the airfield. "We are still boiling water" he reported later when asked for news.

On another occasion I had taken a wrong turning on a taxiway at Toronto and subsequently lost a few places in the queue for take-off. Once airborne I calculated that I would still arrive on schedule at London airport if permitted to cruise at Mach point eight six, but after a time I received instructions to reduce speed to avoid overtaking a Boeing at the same flight level and on the same track as myself. I used the public address system to explain this fact to the passengers and added that in consequence we would arrive about fifteen minutes late into London. Back came a note from one of our Boeing captains who was travelling as a passenger. He had not failed to observe my error on the ground at Toronto. "If you had not lost yourself before we got airborne," he wrote, "we would never have been behind that Boeing."

When a sufficient number of Super VC10s had been delivered services to Detroit and Chicago were taken over from the Boeing flight. Eventually a daily service was introduced leaving London each morning and crews found themselves back home in under forty-eight hours. In years gone by a former director of medical services for B.O.A.C. had recommended two local nights rest after an Atlantic crossing. The trip had then taken very much longer but there remained the additional awkward ajustment to a time change of six hours. With the advent of the jets the two local nights were traded away in one of the regular rounds of negotiation between management and pilots. Each day a crew from London arrived at Chicago at four p.m. when it was ten p.m. in England. Although ready for bed they would invariably wake up at two or three o'clock in the morning if they turned in as soon as they arrived at the hotel. In fact the body's rhythm is such that those who stayed up until nine or ten o'clock local time also woke in the early hours and found it difficult to obtain further sleep. Early in the afternoon they were collected and flew through the night back to London.

Conversely another crew which had originally left London at the same time in the morning but flying east to Bombay or Karachi found that the locals were all abed when they arrived. When they woke it was nearer lunchtime than breakfast but they were truly refreshed.

The Britannias were retired from passenger service in 1964 and were sold to the independent companies. They had established a superb safety record and years later many of them were still flying passengers on their summer holidays to the Mediterranean and further afield. Thus the last propeller-driven aircraft left the service of B.O.A.C. The Comets continued until late in 1965 and then they too were sold. Both types had flown for seven years and had been well liked by pilots and passengers for their safety and dependability. The Comet IV had been able to show in unexpected ways the strength of its construction. On one occasion an aircraft approaching Rome's Fiumicino airport at night tuned in and descended towards the local approach beacon. Unfortunately another very powerful transmitter in Europe on the same frequency deflected the pilot's director needle, luring him off course and towards more hilly terrain. Rome airport is at sea level very near the coast and its approaches are not obstructed by high ground. During descent the pilot switched on his lights and was appalled to see the tops of trees illuminated in the powerful beams. Thrusting forward the throttles he climbed away but smacked through the uppermost branches. That aircraft landed safely. Another Comet, its landing gear already lowered preparatory to a night landing at Madrid airport struck a ridge of high ground about six miles from the airport. The undercarriage was smashed and the force of the impact activated some of the crash switches which cut off the fuel to two engines. The captain was able to make a smooth belly landing on the runway and after repairs that aircraft was flown back to England.

De Havilland Comet IV in flight.                                             *British Airways*

An improper setting on the altimeter has caused numerous incidents and accidents throughout the years and the reason is easy to find. At the cruising levels of the modern airliner the subscale on the altimeter is set to 1013 millibars, a purely arbitrary setting to avoid collisions. Descending to his destination the pilot passes through a transition level applicable to that airfield and is informed of the local Q.N.H.* which when set on his altimeter will cause it to read the airfield's true height above mean sea level on touchdown: but the pilot may be required to make his approach to the runway on instruments in fog, low cloud or driving rain and his authorised break-off height for the approach may be as low as 200 feet. He does not want to do mental arithmetic to establish exactly when he is at 200 feet above an airfield 1,585 feet above sea level. If he does not see the runway before him at 200 feet he has to climb instantaneously. So another setting, Q.F.E.*, must be set prior to landing and on touchdown the altimeter will read zero feet.

One night in February 1964 a Comet was descending for a landing at Nairobi airport which is situated more than five thousand feet above mean sea level. The first officer who was handling the controls was required by the company instructions then in force to set Q.F.E. The captain, busy with approach and landing checks, set Q.N.H. The first officer had to fly and to wind the altimeter knob an interminable time to adjust to the Q.F.E. The correct figure was 839 millibars. At 938 millibars he obtained a visual appreciation of the number he had heard repeated to him and stopped winding. He had tuned in his I.L.S. for approach and descent guidance and he noted that this showed him to be too low although his altimeter, over-reading by 3,000 feet, suggested that he was too high. The runway lights merged into a continous line in the distance before him. Arresting his descent too late the aircraft ran along the ground for a few seconds before the captain applied full power to the engines and climbed up. The aircraft landed safely some minutes later.

Naturally a thorough investigation always follows incidents such as these both at company level and often by the government authority where they occur. Indeed a carelessly driven catering or loading vehicle scratching and denting the aircraft's hull is a matter for enquiry and action at company level. In the incidents at Rome and Madrid radio difficulties and an inadequate let down chart were partly the cause. The event at Nairobi was viewed far more seriously. The travelling public expect an airline and its employees to demand of themselves extremely high standards of safety and competence in their operations. Even so there were lessons to be learned. Thereafter both pilots were required to set their altimeters to Q.F.E. for landing and a third altimeter was installed to be set at Q.N.H. In addition a fast winder was attached to the altimeter to obtain rapid change to Q.F.E. at the late and busy time when it must be set.

Ten years later confusion over the aircraft's altitude was the cause of another alarming incident on the approach to Nairobi. The pilots had set their altimeters so that on landing they would read the airfield height above sea level. They misheard instructions from the controller to descend to 7,500 feet and believed that they had been cleared to 5,500 feet which is approximately the height of the airfield. Descending in cloud over hills several miles from the runway they caught a glimpse of ground less than 100 feet below the aircraft and climbed up just in time to avoid disaster. At the subsequent inquiry the captain

*The altimeter is merely an aneroid barometer with the scale graduated in feet (or metres) of height instead of in millibars (or inches of mercury). Movement of the pointers is controlled by variations of pressure. The altimeter is provided with a knob to allow corrections to be made to the pressure.

accepted the blame. He had fallen into the trap of supposing that his altimeter was showing the height of the aircraft above the ground. His resignation was accepted.

*      *      *      *      *      *

Thirty years ago airliners did not usually fly above 10,000 feet because there was seldom any provision of oxygen for the passengers. In the 1950s aircraft with pressurised cabins enabled us to fly at 20,000 feet and higher on the turbine powered Britannias. The Boeing 707 and the VC10 cruise most economically above 30,000 feet and are equipped with radar. This has made it easier for pilots to avoid thunderstorms but there remains an invisible hazard, one which the weather men are seldom able to predict—clear air turbulence.

Jet airliners are flown near the upper level of their operating ceiling to save fuel and increase their range. Whilst the stalling speed of the aircraft increases with altitude the maximum permissible speed decreases and if an airliner is cruising at a moderately heavy weight the safe speed range within which the pilot must fly may be as little as fifty knots. This is not a problem in calm conditions; it is sufficient when the pilot, forewarned by visible evidence of trouble to come, turns on the seat belt sign and cockpit lighting, tightens his harness, selects any necessary de-icing equipment, orders loose equipment in the galleys and elsewhere to be stowed and awaits the expected buffeting. But if in clear skies there is sudden and unexpectedly severe turbulence and the airspeed is allowed to fall too low the aircraft will become unstable and if the stall is penetrated to any depth there may be a considerable loss of height. Should the nose pitch down and the aircraft develop excessive speed it will be subject to severe structural stresses.

On a fine day Mount Fuji in Japan is a beautiful sight, but pilots familiar with the area are wary of approaching it. More than one aircraft has crashed on the lower slopes and the only explanation appeared to be an upset in turbulence. One day in March 1966 a Boeing 707 of B.O.A.C. took off from Tokyo. The weather was perfect and either to save time or to please a full load of passengers the pilot elected to leave the usual airway and headed towards the mountain. A camera was subsequently recovered from the wreckage and the

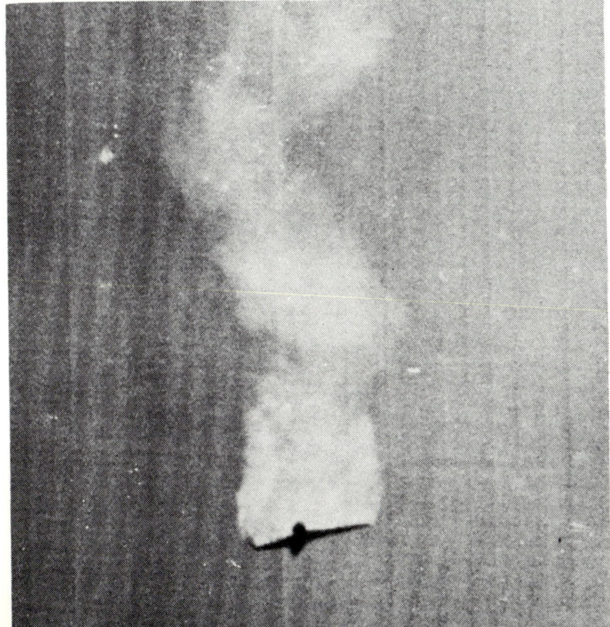

A view of the Boeing 707 after shedding its tail plunging towards Mount Fuji.
*British Airways*

film within it was successfully printed. The camera had been directed at Mount Fuji and the film showed that the photographer had experienced increasing difficulty in holding it steady. Finally the camera fell from his hands. The investigators discovered that the air currents had imposed sufficiently severe loads on the tailplane to cause a structural failure after which the Boeing went into a dive from which recovery was impossible. All on board lost their lives. There have been occasions when pilots have lost control of their aircraft in severe thunderstorms. This was the first "jet upset" in a cloudless sky.

In 1967 the international traveller could expect to be carried on a jet aircraft on all but local or domestic routes. The switch to air travel was a blow to the shipping companies whose finest and proudest vessels were either taken out of service or plied their trade on winter cruises. Even those so long faithful to the *Queens* had joined the "jet set".

Yet the airlines were anxious to demonstrate that flying was not merely the prerogative of the wealthy and successful. Less often were seen advertisements displaying elegant passengers in an aura of first class luxury, temporarily diverted from their champagne and Remy Martin by the appearance of the captain, graciously pointing out the Great Pyramid, clearly visible and apparently only a few hundred feet below the starboard wing tip.

All had changed. Heralded by the warning cry of "Passengers!" from the traffic officer or a less respectful call of "Here come the punters!" from one of their own number the stewards and stewardesses composed themselves to meet the oncoming horde, as ordinary looking as those at any bus or rail terminal, but often encumbered with parcels or packages far exceeding reasonable proportions. Certainly one carried royal personages from time to time, frequently there were diplomats and the aristocrats of commerce. There were also miserable deportees, shuttling to and fro between London and the East African countries which were the only home they had known. Occasionally there would be a prisoner under guard and from time to time an unfortunate passenger on a stretcher, partly hidden from view by curtains and attended by a doctor or nurse.

Old rules prohibiting cigar and pipe-smoking had been abandoned. The non-smoker could only hope not to be surrounded by the addicts until such time in the future when airlines were able to allocate a non-smoking zone of seats. A scheme to allow passengers to choose their seat sometimes caused raised voices when the boarding passenger found his promised seat occupied by someone else. There were tears and wails when there were more infants than could be accommodated in the special cots.

These are problems that a good chief steward will attend to and overcome but sometimes a furious traveller demands to speak to the captain. Most airlines carry passenger comment cards but these are often declined by those who prefer to have their say there and then to someone in authority. Considerable diplomacy has to be exercised when one or more passengers come on board having imbibed too freely in the airport bar. The official Air Navigation Regulations state clearly that travellers "under the influence" shall not be carried. The airlines are of course fearful of lawsuits by indignant passengers who have paid their fare, perhaps waited some hours for a delayed flight and are then barred from flying. Company regulations recommend the captain to obtain a medical opinion and written comments from witnesses before refusing such a passenger. Consequently it is usually necessary to carry them but further alcoholic refreshment in the air can be withheld.

When everyone is on board and the aircraft has begun its journey to the take off point tower controllers in some overseas countries ask the pilot to notify the number of "souls on board". Usually they mean the absolute total but a few countries exclude the crew from the count of souls. The airlines use the abbreviation "pax" but occasionally a coffin is carried in the hold and the load sheet may refer to "human remains" or even "cadaver". Many years ago I witnessed a tragi-comic scene on a boiling hot day on an African airfield. A little band of respectful loaders, supervised by one European traffic officer brought out to my aircraft the coffin of a colleague to be flown to Britain for burial. The hold was already very full and without a fork lift or any modern lifting apparatus they encountered enormous difficulty in stowing the coffin in the confined space available. Tipped this way and that it barked shins, skinned knuckles and crushed toes. Stilled voices had risen to vibrant shouts and the tempers of all were distinctly frayed by the time their task was at last completed. No lingering traces of reverence remained. The traffic officer had the final say. "Funny thing," he remarked as he signed the load sheet. "In life that chap could be a thoroughly awkward blighter."

Once the aircraft is on its way with the stewards and stewardesses taking orders for drinks or serving meals the nervous passengers observe the children undismayed, infants lulled to sleep by the steady drone, the general air of normalcy. Those who have never flown before are also reassured. From time to time passengers are so pleased with the treatment they have received and the general conduct of their flight that they write to the airline to express their appreciation and when names are mentioned the individual may receive a copy of their complimentary letter. I have a very few of these and it is pleasant to keep them.

To the best of my knowledge only one passenger has written to point the finger of complaint directly at myself. The specific cause of his indignation was one landing "with an almighty crash". Someone in the public relations department had written a mollifying reply which failed to appease him so he followed his first letter with another for the personal attention of the chairman. We all make hard landings at times but rough ones are not necessarily unsafe. A landing on a very wet runway, especially if it is combined with a strong crosswind, calls for a firm touchdown and one rudder pedal depressed at just the right moment to kick off the drift. A pilot who tried to "grease" his aircraft on to the runway in such conditions could find himself off the edge of the runway and on to the grass in no time. Captains must share the flying with junior pilots and new recruits are obviously less experienced. The occasional hard landing is inevitable but pilots tend to be perfectionists and curse themselves as heartily for their misjudgements as those golfers who fluff their putts.

Some of the letters received are quite remarkable. I was once shown one in which the writer insisted that he had glanced through the opened crew door and had observed no one but a stewardess in occupation of the cockpit, no pilots at all although he conceded that the door might have obscured the flight engineer at his station. It must require considerable ingenuity to answer such accusations to the satisfaction of the recipient.

All travellers abroad like to bring home articles which are either scarce or unobtainable or merely different. After the war when rationing had continued for some years in Britain crews had brought eggs, fruit, hams and canned goods. Even rugs and carpets had found their way back in the aircraft holds and of course one was always being asked to bring home nylon stockings for female friends and relatives. When these things became freely available other items became prized purchases. In the nineteen fifties "My Fair Lady" was a smash hit on Broadway and ran there for several years before it arrived at Drury Lane. The long-playing record of the various musical scores was not permitted to be sold in England until the show opened. This record more than any other was in great demand. Later on the small transistor radio was available in Japan and the United States long before it was imported into Britain.

There is little that one cannot obtain at home today although watches, tape-recorders and similar items may be more cheaply purchased in Singapore or Hong Kong. Crews still arrive home with fruit, particularly avocado pears from Nairobi. One is less frequently begged to bring something home but occasionally one receives an urgent request to carry a parcel for a friend. One such was John whom I had first met when we attended the same school at the age of seven. Thirty years or so later he was temporarily attached to the U.K. Mission to the United Nations in New York. As I was about to fly there I telephoned to his wife whom he had left behind in Twickenham and offered to convey a message. In turn she begged me to drive over and collect from her one pot of his favourite marmalade. Hoping to complete some gardening chore before my departure I played for time by consulting my wife.

"Your oldest friend! Of course we will both go over and take the poor girl out to lunch." The next day therefore I had the marmalade with me as I flew to New York and I arrived wearily in the hotel at a time when the English were all abed. I rang my friend. "Come over," he insisted. "If you walk as far as Columbus Circle you won't have to change twice on the subway." When the marmalade had finally changed hands I was unable to resist remarking that the particular brand was available at more than one chain of stores in New York. "Oh, I know," he replied, "but think of the enormous pleasure it will have given the dear girl to have sent this gift all that way by you."

The customs officers at all the world's airports are not concerned with pots of marmalade. Some exercise themselves with a search for drugs, others grow frenzied at the sight of *Playboy* magazine, a few seize with puritan horror anything containing alcohol. The experienced traveller soon learns how the game is played. In Britain and the U.S.A. crew members are dealt with apart from the general public. We have always found the Americans easy-going. At home it has been the practice for many years for the crews to write out a list of purchases on a special form of declaration. The customs officer peruses it before releasing the crew. It has always been a matter of annoyance that we are less generously treated than the businessman or holidaymaker who has been abroad for a couple of days. He is allowed a bottle of spirits and a carton of cigarettes, duty free. The crew member has to be abroad for eight days before even a half bottle may be imported.

# CHAPTER TEN

# The Changing View from the Flight Deck

SIR Giles Guthrie had become chairman when the fortunes of B.O.A.C. were on the upturn after one of the periodic recessions which afflict the airlines like any other business. With an all-jet fleet the company was in good shape to handle the increasing business and aircraft were travelling with few empty seats. But when Sir Charles Hardie took over at the end of 1968 he inherited a seething dispute between the Corporation and the pilots.

The pilots' union, B.A.L.P.A., had been in existence since 1937 but apart from a general secretary no permanent negotiators or professional adivsers were employed and the conduct of affairs was undertaken by pilots in their free time. This policy was based on the belief that laymen did not understand the problems of airmen. With the advantage of hindsight it is clear that our reluctance to engage full-time professional negotiators had unfortunate consequences. In 1968 the salaries of B.O.A.C. pilots were lower than those of any other major European airline with the exception of the Irish. The upshot was the first strike by British pilots since the formation of Imperial Airways out of a number of companies in 1921.

Today hospital consultants and doctors are prepared to defy the Minister of Health but at that time there was some surprise at the pilots' action and press comment was generally unfavourable. After the strike was settled some of those who had found temporary employment had amusing tales to tell. One man was seen on television in charge of an enormous lorry. The interviewer blandly inquired whether such work differed greatly from flying an aeroplane. "It is less arduous," viewers were informed. "By law I am required to stop driving after eleven hours on the road, but in an aircraft I am sometimes expected to remain on duty for fifteen hours."

Another pilot attracted the attention of the press when his fellow workers in a factory making mattresses complained that his output greatly exceeded their normal quota and asked the management to sack him. During the stoppage I worked with four other pilots, building a huge shed for occupation by turkeys. Our employer paid us generously on an hourly basis and the shed was approaching completion when the strike came to an end.

Since those days B.A.L.P.A. has been reorganised. Industrial advisers have been engaged to serve under a general secretary who is among the highest paid executives of any British trades union. Determined not to lose the ground gained B.A.L.P.A. likes to project a strong image and proclamations issuing from the headquarters near London Airport are sometimes couched in aggressive terms. To me it seems rather sad that communication with one's employer should be conducted in the manner of an estranged couple who exchange messages in writing. Many will say that it is inevitable. B.O.A.C. and B.E.A. each of which numbered over 20,000 employees, have merged to form British Airways and the management has inevitably become even more remote from the workforce than it was before.

There have been other changes. Some of us used to fly with a second pilot, a navigator, a radio operator and a flight engineer in an aircraft which seated less than a tenth of the passengers currently carried in a widebodied jet. In the last thirty years aircraft have grown much bigger but the flight crew has been reduced to two or three men. Airlines have been able to carry more passengers without employing more pilots but the competition between carriers has become very fierce. For reasons of prestige a newly independent country forms its own national airline and is prepared to operate at a considerable loss. In Britain each passing year has seen one or more independent companies defeated by the ruthless competition and forced out of business. There is always a pool of unemployed pilots.

A different situation exists in the passenger cabin where the number of attendants has increased. Stewardesses first appeared on British airliners in 1946 and initially there was only one among the crew. On flights overseas on a trip which might take several weeks she was uniquely placed to enjoy the attentions of her male companions. As time went by two or three stewardesses were carried and in recent years a much greater number to look after several hundred passengers on the largest airliners. The older flyer addicted to temporary romantic attachments readily admits that this profusion of female company has come too late. Today it is the dashing young co-pilot, currently well able to afford a modern sports car who is best placed to make the running. "Mummy asked to be remembered to you," a charming new recruit informed me. "She used to fly with you on Argonauts."

The first stewardesses whom B.O.A.C. employed were supplied with stiff white collars and black ties worn under military style jackets decorated with clusters of brass buttons. Then open-necked blouses were introduced while skirt length followed current fashion. When the hem of the mini-skirt reached its greatest distance from ground level some startling sights compelled the attention of even the most jaded passengers packed like sardines into the economy cabin. The duties of a stewardess involve considerable stretching and stooping. There are items to be stowed in overhead racks and it is a long arm's length to pass a tray across two other passengers to those seated by the windows. The traveller occasionally found himself an eye-boggling six inches from areas of girl not normally seen in public.

In some parts of the world the mini-skirt is banned by law. When our aircraft landed in Malawi stewardesses were not permitted to disembark until a traffic clerk had appeared on board with matching maxi-skirts to cover their exposed limbs. Of course all airlines aim to clothe their girls in attractive uniforms and one of the most pleasing sights I have seen are the stewardesses of a Japanese airline wearing national costume. It cannot be a practical uniform in an aircraft cabin but I rejoice in the recollection of one such group assembling in the foyer of our hotel and bowing to one another.

For some time past a number of Asian stewardesses have worked among our cabin staff to assist passengers originating from Hong Kong or Japan, India and Pakistan. They get on well with their British colleagues and many of them become surprisingly anglicised. At the airport at Bombay my crew were being pestered by urchins begging for the ballpoint pens which many airlines hand out to passengers. Expecting her to address them in their own tongue I asked an Indian stewardess to send them away. Stepping forward she raised a threatening arm. From her lips came two commanding words. " Piss off!"

The first airline to put the Boeing 747, popularly known as the Jumbo, into service was Pan American Airways. B.O.A.C. had ordered some but the initial batch which were delivered did not carry any passengers for over a year. The reason was a dispute about how many pilots were required to fly the machine and the salary they should receive. Ultimately there was agreement and today two pilots and an engineer occupy the flight deck. Navigation is by the inertial system known as I.N.S. which gives an instant reading of the aircraft's latitude and longitude, ground speed, wind direction and velocity, drift and crosstrack error. The sextant and Loran set have disappeared along with plotting charts and astronomical tables. To eliminate ambiguity three I.N.S. sets are installed and to assist the pilot on an approach in conditions of low cloud or poor visibility three automatic pilots can be coupled to an automatic landing system.

A Boeing 747 crosses the runway threshold. *British Airways*

Above: vapour trails from a Boeing 747 in flight and below: a Boeing 747 at touchdown.    *British Airways*

The cost of the I.N.S. sets is very high, too great to justify their installation on machines due to be phased out within a short time. It is also very expensive to convert pilots from one type to another and captains within a few years of retirement were not permitted to transfer to the Boeing 747. This did not worry those of us who enjoyed flying the VC10 and knew that it would remain in service for as long if not longer than ourselves. Another good reason for remaining on the VC10 was the wide variety of pleasant places including islands and resorts which we visited. Inevitably the Boeing 747 began by serving cities like New York and Montreal where passengers were forthcoming in sufficient numbers to provide an adequate payload.

The provision of I.N.S. eliminated the principal function of the third pilot who had navigated over oceans and deserts. An increasing number of radio beacons have been installed on airways routes across the most barren and unpopulated areas and the third pilot was left with little to do except during the busy take-off and landing phase when he monitored the actions of the captain and co-pilot. During the cruise he might read a book or wander back into the galley to chat up the stewardess. The story is told of one such man who had been explaining to a passenger the division of duties on the flight deck. "So what do you do?" the passenger enquired. The third pilot was not lost for an answer. "I am the captain's sexual adviser," he explained. "I watch what he is doing and if I offer any suggestions he reminds me that when he wants my effing opinion he will ask for it."

When I am informed that a former airline pilot is among my passengers it is a pleasure to invite him into the cockpit. Such men are always interested in new aircraft which have entered service since they retired. There must still be a few contemporaries of Antoine de St Exupery, celebrated author of *Wind, Sand and Stars* who was a pilot with the French company which fifty years ago flew the mail to West Africa, across the Atlantic to Brazil and through the passes of the Andes mountains to Chile. We, their successors, no longer sit in heavy leather clothing, listening to the beat of the propellers and the whine of the windstream against the struts. Nor can we open a window and peer through goggles at an unwelcome slick of oil streaming back from an engine. We do not sit, map in hand and attempt to fix the aircraft's position by reference to a landmark momentarily visible through a break in the clouds. As aviation has developed the airline pilot has come to depend more and more upon information presented to him inside the cockpit, not only during the cruise but all the way down to the runway.

About thirty years ago an American pilot Ernest Gann retired from airline flying and became a successful author. *Fate is the Hunter* is a record of his experiences. At that time it was often impossible to avoid flying in icing conditions. One entered thick banks of cloud illuminated only by flashes of lightning and prayed that one's passage through it would be swift and not too rough. Piston engines had improved and the pilot could adjust the pitch of his propellers but the numerous gauges on the engine panel were a reminder of how many things could go wrong.

The old-timer might think that the airline pilots of today are a spoiled lot. We sit in seats with armrests and are allowed to smoke a cigarette. We wear no special helmet and are unconcerned by an outside air temperature gauge which frequently records a figure too

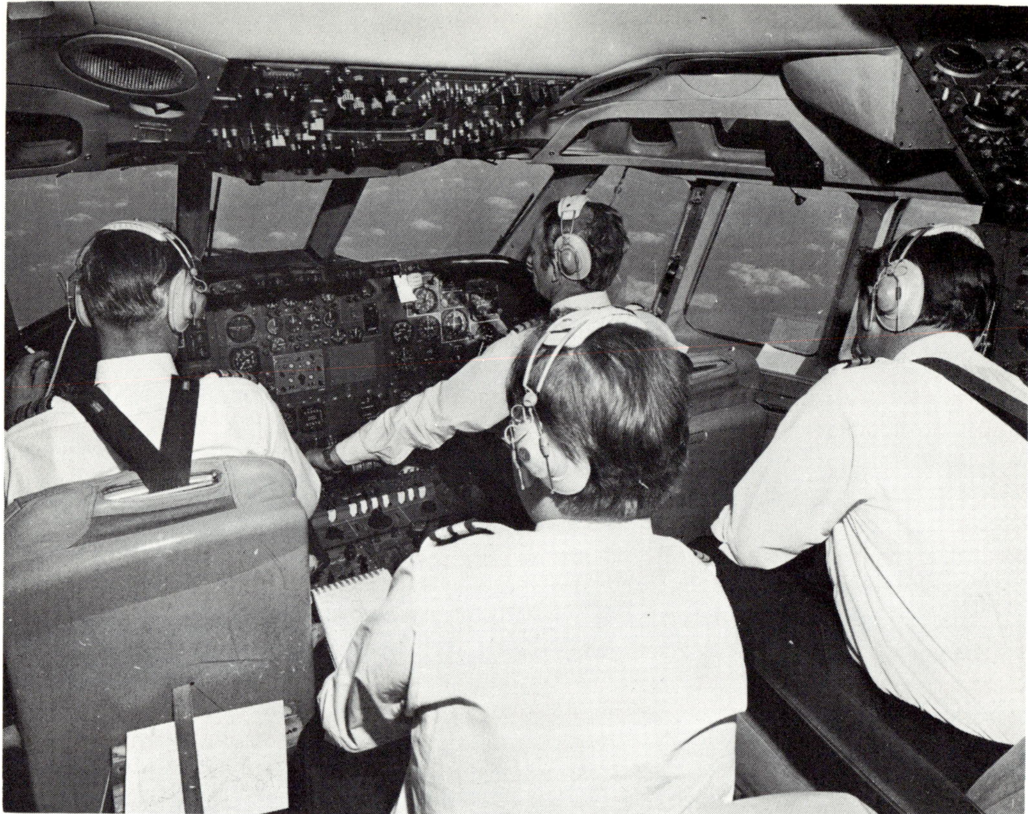

The third pilot (nearest camera) monitors the actions of the other pilots.　　*British Airways*

low for human survival. On the other hand we do have to contend with a few problems which he did not meet.

His take-off was not delayed by a long line of other machines ahead of his own in the queue. There were so few other aircraft in the sky that he was able to alter the altitude and direction of his own machine as and when he liked. He was accompanied by a wireless operator to obtain his weather reports and he did not have to listen to a constant flow of instructions only a small part of which were of concern to himself. He would be surprised to learn how small a reserve of fuel we carry these days and when the weather at his destination was quite good enough for a landing he was not required to join a stack of other aircraft and await his turn to descend.

He might scoff at these observations. He might point at the multiple autopilots with fingertip control of altitude and heading; the automatic throttles with provision for the pilot to select an airspeed; the heated windscreen and duplicated electrical and hydraulic systems. One might sense his impression that we have only to watch the aeroplane fly itself. But together with all this equipment are dozens of warning devices, red lights, bells, horns and failure flags to demand a positive action by the pilot when something goes wrong.

If he listened to the flow of instructions issued to the modern pilot on an approach to a major airport he would be amazed how much authority has been surrendered to controllers on the ground and he would recall the occasions when he had found his way into airports using his own skill and cunning in the days when radar was unknown and radio direction finding a primitive art. In present circumstances our dependence upon ground control has occasionally lulled pilots into a sense of false security and a few have forgotten that an instruction to descend does not remove from the captain his responsibility for flying at a safe altitude above high ground.

The discussion may turn to airports and the advantages of runways over grass fields but just as the proud owners of powerful new motor cars deplore the speed restrictions necessary on winding and poorly surfaced roads so flying men fret at the failure of the responsible authorities to match the facilities of the airports with the needs of each new generation of aircraft. Many runways are too short and taxiways too narrow; lighting is poor and instrument landing systems are wrongly sited or not provided. Consequently the airlines are reluctant to operate their new aeroplanes into some of the stations along the line, particularly in bad weather.

Some of the busiest airports in Europe and North America have already reached the limit of expansion. London Airport was intended to have six runways and five were actually completed around buildings sited in the centre and connected to the nearest road by tunnel. As the number of travellers increased extra buildings could only be provided by encroaching upon the runways. Today three runways remain and two are sited parallel with one another. The third one is too short for an airliner carrying the amount of fuel necessary for an Atlantic crossing and delays are caused when a wind in excess of thirty knots is blowing at right angles across the parallel runways.

It is difficult for a poor country to afford the equipment essential to an airport and a backward country does not have sufficient men trained to keep delicate instruments in working order. The airport which serves a nation's capital is likely to be the best equipped while others visited only by the domestic carrier are often primitive. This presents a problem to the international airlines which must recommend to their captains airports suitable for a diversion. The pilot of a Boeing 707 looks for a runway with a minimum length of 7,000 feet and 150 feet is the standard width.

Easter Island in the Pacific ocean has an airfield whose sole runway lies between hills and has a pronounced slope. It measures 6,600 by 91 feet. The Boeings of LAN-Chile land there but only during the hours of daylight. Some time ago an Australian flew along with the obliging Chileans to assess the airport's suitability as an alternate on the Pacific network of Quantas and Air New Zealand. He was horrified by the difficulties an approach would present to a crew unfamiliar with the island. "It would be safer to ditch in the sea," he said.

Quite a different situation is found in the Sheikhdoms of the Gulf of Arabia where

<br>

**British airways**    **FLIGHT OPERATIONS UNIT  LONDON**
Overseas Division

**Airport Briefing** ________________________

| ISSUED | | REFERENCE | | CANCELS | |
|---|---|---|---|---|---|
| 27/1200 | | 6S/CMC/2283 | | 6S/MA/2268 | |

| AIRPORT | | INFORMATION | SOURCE |
|---|---|---|---|
| TANZANIA | | | |
| DAR-ES-SALAAM | R/WY 05 | VASIS U/S. | HKNA 425 5/7 |
| | TAR | U/S. | HKNA 109 19/2 |
| | R/WY 23 | VASIS U/S. | HKNA 473 26/7 |
| | VOR | U/S. | HKNA 432 9/7 |
| KILIMANJARO | TAR | U/S. | HKNA 259 14/4 |
| | VOR | 'KV' 113.8  U/S. | HKNA 471 25/7 |
| | DME | U/S. | HKNA 472 25/7 |

Briefing sheet for flight crews showing unserviceability of Visual Approach Slope Indicators, Terminal Approach Radar, and Distance Measurement Equipment at Tanzania's two airports.

money is plentiful and urban development does not encroach upon acres of sand surrounding the airports. Runways of enormous length have been built to accommodate both wide-bodied jets and the Concorde. Dubai has a splendid air-conditioned terminal building which, topped with domes and minarets, looks like the fulfillment of a dream, a storybook palace. It is very different from the tents, the windsock and the oil slicks on the hard sand which marked the landing grounds in that region thirty years ago.

Some of the oil producing countries have formed their own airlines and operate international services. The upsurge of Arab nationalism has been accompanied by a revival of strict religious observance and the airlines of Saudi Arabia and Kuwait no longer serve alcoholic drinks to passengers. Indeed some of the Gulf states impose very severe penalties on passengers who attempt to smuggle in wines and spirits. Fortunately members of airline crews have long been accepted as infidels beyond hope of redemption and even when our baggage has been scrutinised by X-ray equipment revealing all too clearly some familiar shapes the customs officers, impassive in their flowing white robes, raise their eyes to the Prophet, sigh for our damned souls and wave us through.

All too often some bizarre local wrangle can disrupt aircraft movements. Our VC10 arrived at an African airport. There were two more stops to be made, the second at the Seychelles, which had just celebrated its independence. After checking the flight plan I was notified that a diplomatic dispute about traffic rights was certain to delay our departure.

The East African Community, the organisation which employed the air traffic controllers, insisted that British Airways no longer possessed the rights to accept local passengers bound for the sovereign independent Seychelles republic. The E.A.C. representative instructed the men in the control tower to refuse me a clearance. The company traffic officer rang up the British High Commission who tried to find the appropriate cabinet minister.

On board the aircraft more than a hundred passengers who had made the overnight journey from London remained in their seats, prohibited from disembarking for reasons of security. Even the uniformed customs officer who had mounted the steps to carry out his routine checks of the ship's papers and bonded stores had been denied entrance by a zealous guard for failing to wear his approved identity pass.

Time went by and it became very warm. No air conditioning truck was available. Apologies and explanations were offered to the perspiring passengers. At last the Minister for Tourism was himself found to be in the departure lounge. Apprised of the problem he indignantly refuted the E.A.C.'s overriding authority over his own office and warned the men in the control tower that unless they wanted to end up in a prison cell they had better issue me a clearance. "Yes, Minister," they chorused in unison.

But the customs formalities had still to be completed and an officer was begged to come on board, with or without his identity pass, to do the necessary. A smirk on his face he took his time about it. The joining passengers boarded just as the fuel in the ground-start truck ran out, extinguishing all the lights, shutting off even the pitiful jets of air above each seat. More apologies were offered to the weary passengers.

We took off nearly two hours late and I recorded these events in the voyage report log. I thought of all the other occasions when I had been delayed at such places and I added another sentence. Normal transit of an African station.

All airlines are concerned about their safety record and pilots support measures to protect themselves and their passengers. A flight recorder, often referred to in newspapers as the "black box", has been fitted on airliners for a number of years and when recovered after an accident has provided vital clues to assist the investigators. More recently a cockpit voice recorder has been introduced. This enables the last thirty minutes of conversation on the flight deck to be played back.

Some airline pilots had reservations about the use of recorders. They accepted the need to know why accidents had occurred but feared that government or company inspectors would examine the tapes to study their conduct of ordinary day to day operations. It must be remembered that our competency is put to the test several times each year and a failed check means the withdrawal of our licence, a second failure the probable loss of employment. A compromise was reached. Many airlines do scrutinise the tapes of the flight recorder and note excessive rates of descent or exceptional speeds achieved on take-off or landing. They may publish details of variations from standard operating practice in notices to their crews but normally do not identify and interrogate the responsible pilot. In the case of the cockpit voice recorder all conversation on the tape is erased by the pilot at the conclusion of each uneventful flight. To do this he has only to press a button.

The requirements of safety must override any inhibitions aircrews may have about these recorders but few people would willingly allow their private conversation to become the property of third parties. On the route to Japan there is a change of crew in Moscow. A convivial party was under way in one of the hotel bedrooms. Someone expressed the hope that the room was not bugged, whereupon those present decided to carry out a thorough investigation, peering behind the pictures hung upon the walls and examining the fixtures and fittings. When it was noticed that the floor beneath the carpet was slightly uneven in one small area the carpet was rolled back to reveal a circular disc held in place by four screws. The flight engineer was urged to loosen each screw. The task was almost complete when a resounding crash was heard. The chandelier in the room beneath them was totally destroyed.

One form of communication has vastly improved over the years. Aircraft sometimes arrived over an airfield before the local staff had received a departure signal from the last stop and messages listing maintenance or catering requirements frequently failed to arrive. Because aircraft have often been parked at a considerable distance from the company office the traffic officer had to make several long journeys before he was satisfied that all was ready for the boarding of passengers. Today many airlines have allotted to them a frequency in the V.H.F. band for the exchange of messages with their aircraft and we can also communicate with headquarters on certain frequencies on the H.F. band when we are thousands of miles away.

On the V.H.F. band there is a frequency reserved solely for aircraft in distress. Over oceans and deserts we monitor this but do not use it lightly. Non-essential chatter is likely to be interrupted by an irate pilot. "Get off this channel. Someone may need it." I have yet to hear anyone in very serious trouble broadcasting over the distress frequency but I have listened on H.F. to a pilot relaying the demands of armed men to his company headquarters.

The last chairman of B.O.A.C. before that Corporation and B.E.A. were merged into British Airways was Sir Keith Granville. Unlike his predecessors he had worked his way to the top after joining as an apprentice more than thirty years earlier. During his term of office we were faced with a new problem—hijacking.

The history of violence by individuals and more notably by extremist organisations against airline passengers and crews has already been the subject of several books. Every day numerous airports in the Middle East are visited by our VC10s and we have the dubious distinction of being three times the target of Palestinian guerillas. The first such attack took place in September 1970. About a hundred passengers, many of them children returning to school in Britain were on the aircraft when the cockpit door burst open and the barrel of a gun was pressed into the neck of the captain. Forced to land at a disused airstrip in Jordan the occupants of the aircraft spent several uncomfortable days and nights before

The charred remains of a B.O.A.C. VC10, Swissair DC8 and T.W.A. Boeing 707 after their destruction by Palestinian terrorists.

*British Airways*

the majority of them were released and the VC10 blown up. The flight crew and some selected passengers remained prisoners of the guerillas for several weeks.

Despite the introduction of security measures a second VC10 was hijacked to Amsterdam, a grenade being held at the throat of the pilot. This aircraft too was destroyed. Late in 1974 a third VC10 was taken over by armed intruders during a transit stop in Dubai. This time there were human casualties, a stewardess and a loader who were shot during the initial attack and a passenger who was deliberately murdered before the eyes of the authorities at Tunis Airport where the guerillas had diverted the aircraft and made a number of demands.

Tunis, November 1974. Stretcher bearers remove corpse of passenger murdered by hijackers of a VC10.
Associated Press

Measures to combat hijacking vary. El Al, the Israeli airline, provide their crews with pistols and carry armed guards with instructions to resist any attack. Conversely many other airlines instruct their crews to do everything possible to protect the lives of passengers even if this means obeying instructions issued by the hijackers. But to prevent this type of criminal from boarding an aeroplane passengers are at present subjected to a personal search. That these measures have proved an effective deterrent is shown by several attempts to fire upon aircraft from airport buildings.

Extra security staff have been engaged to ensure that employees of catering or other trades do not hide weapons on board for use by a travelling gang. There have been occasions when a passage has been booked by someone who has checked in a bag but not boarded the aircraft. An explosion in mid-air has followed. Consequently captains are most reluctant to depart when a head-count reveals that a passenger is missing, one whose bag must be presumed to be stowed in the hold. Sometimes it has been necessary to remove every item of luggage and ask each passenger to identify his own property. Tempers fray when this tedious checking reveals a clerical error, a bewildered old lady who has forgotten her flight number or an unrepentant tippler still seated in the airport bar.

My crew replaced another at Kuala Lumpur and the passengers, many of whom had begun their journey in Australia, returned on board when refuelling was completed. All were counted and someone was found to be missing. Names were checked against the manifest and at last the absentee was identified as one D. Bass. "Oh!" exclaimed a passenger. "That must surely be my double bass fiddle. I bought a ticket for it to avoid the risk of damage if it was placed in the hold." Mr D. Bass had begun the journey on the seat adjoining his owner but when a lavatory went out of order a steward had installed the instrument and locked the door. There Mr Bass remained mute and uncomplaining, unaware that we were investigating something more sinister than a fiddle.

On another occasion I landed in Jamaica en route from Mexico City to Bermuda. The airport manager took me aside and murmured a few words. "We have reason to believe that someone is trying to plant a package in the hold of your aircraft." He had my entire attention at once. He went on to say that an airport loader had repeatedly made enquiries about the time of arrival of my flight and had incurred the suspicion of his supervisor. After some of the cargo had been loaded we checked the hold and found a carton improperly labelled and consigned to Bermuda. Inside, wrapped in tinfoil and sewn into a jacket, was a quantity of marijuana. Apparently it is not unusual for workers in the cane fields to grow an illicit crop and the loader had an accomplice who worked on the airport in Bermuda where marijuana fetches a very high price.

In the pursuit of safety the investigation of curious happenings may uncover a misdemeanour or result in anti-climax or farce but the menace of the hijacker and the bomber is too serious to treat lightly. Airline crews may appear to accept the situation with calm stoicism but all are disgusted that the most vicious assassins can still find sanctuary in certain parts of the world. Too many governments act in a manner which reflects a bent morality.

A VC10 was flying from London to Khartoum carrying the man chosen as their new President by a military group which had temporarily overthrown the existing regime in the Sudan. The aircraft passed from the control of Malta and entered Libyan air space. Minutes later the Libyan controller ordered the pilot to land at Benina. To avoid compliance with this demand the captain renewed radio contact with Malta and asked to be assigned a route and flight level back to London. The Libyan controller had anticipated this reaction. He warned the captain that refusal to land would imperil the aircraft. Faced with this threat the captain landed at Benina where the president-elect and his aide were forced to disembark. A few days later they were handed over to their enemies in Khartoum and summarily executed.

More fortunate was an Algerian subject who was removed by the Israeli police from one of our aircraft which had made a scheduled stop in Tel Aviv. Although the man was identified as a senior intelligence agent he was eventually released.

The overthrow of the civil government of Uganda by the extraordinary Idi Amin was followed by reprisals against supporters of the former regime and the elimination of any possible rivals. To curry popularity with Africans thousands of citizens of Asian origin were stripped of their possessions and expelled. Uganda had long been popular with foreign tourists and some airlines continued to operate into Entebbe Airport but many visitors found the atmosphere increasingly hostile. It was not uncommon for soldiers to stamp into the bars and rooms of hotels and take away guests of any race or colour. On one occasion they arrested some of our crew members but an alert eye-witness telephoned to the British High Commission who were able to secure their release.

I was in Uganda when a VC10 arrived with some military supplies consigned to Zambia, the ultimate destination of the aircraft. The Ugandans had been notified in advance of the shipment, which was correctly manifested, but Amin seized upon the opportunity to cause trouble. He refused to allow the aircraft to proceed until, in his own words, he was satisfied that the weapons were not to be used against his African brothers. The passengers were removed to a hotel and armed guards posted round their prize. Ordinary legal measures to recover the aircraft in a country whose Chief Justice has been abducted from his own court were useless and diplomatic representations proceeded fruitlessly for several weeks before Amin relented. By this time my crew had been withdrawn and soon after the airlines ceased to lodge their flight personnel in Uganda.

# Conclusion

THOSE of us who served during the Second World War are over fifty years of age and most have already retired from active flying. The survivors, if that is not an inappropriate description, are frequently asked when they expect to retire, particularly by first officers anxious to move across to the left-hand seat. One must sympathise with them. Twenty-five years ago we made similar enquiries about former Imperial Airways captains.

In the United States airline pilots are permitted to fly until their sixtieth birthday but fifty-five is the customary age limit of crew members employed in most British companies. Some pilots elect to leave before this while others are reluctant to give up flying and seek a post with another airline. Those best placed to do this are the possessors of a licence endorsed for a Boeing 707, a type which is in service with a great many companies, throughout the world. On our travels we sometimes see the familiar faces of former colleagues beneath their new and alien headgear.

Some of these men have commanded a far greater variety of aircraft than their contemporaries in foreign airlines and the reason is not hard to find. Britain ended the war with numerous aircraft manufacturers, some of whom turned to the production of civil machines, not only in competition with one another but also with the formidable American industry. Lacking a substantial home market sales of even the best aircraft have been disappointing. B.E.A. consistently bought British aircraft and had a winner in the Viscount but B.O.A.C. burnt its fingers with the Tudor, Hermes and Comet I and relied heavily upon American products. As a result famous old companies like Handley Page have gone out of business whilst De Havilland, Vickers and A. V. Roe have been absorbed into one or other of the two remaining manufacturers of any size, Hawker Siddeley and the British Aircraft Corporation.

Whilst his contemporaries in K.L.M. or an American airline graduated from a Douglas DC3 to a DC4, a DC6 and a DC8 the veteran British pilot may have switched from an Avro York to a Lockheed Constellation then flown a Boeing Stratocruiser, followed by a Hawker Siddeley Comet and a Vickers VC10. But the working life of airline pilots on international routes has followed a similar course. We have flown on parallel tracks and when at night our paths have crossed we have signalled a greeting with our lights. We have relayed position reports for one another when the airwaves have been cluttered by too many voices all speaking at once. We have rubbed shoulders in customs sheds, drunk together in bars and stayed at the same hotels.

The Concorde takes off from London Airport.  *British Airways*

Twenty-five years ago the production of the Comet I was a bold venture which, had it been successful, would have captured for Britain a major share of the market in jet airliners. Sadly the outcome was a tragic failure. Another attempt to take a giant leap forward has been the development of a supersonic transport in conjunction with the French. But while everyone of good will wished the Comet to succeed the progress of the Concorde has been accompanied by a continuing barrage of denigration by all manner of ill-assorted bedfellows. Somehow the manufacturers have been able to carry on and British Airways along with Air France hope to prove the venture successful.

Such an airliner will halve the flying time of the longest journeys. Whatever the delays caused by financial and technical problems or difficulties imposed by political and environmental lobbies one can be sure that a future generation of pilots will fly airliners at twice the speed of those currently in service.

The night sky is familiar to the long distance flyer. I have witnessed many displays of the northern lights—the Aurora Borealis, gazed upon comets, caught glimpses of fireballs and the flare of a meteorite as it re-entered the atmosphere of the earth. I have watched manned satellites traverse the sky. But no one has observed every manifestation of man and nature. A new experience awaits the supersonic traveller. Who will not exclaim in pride and awe at his first sight of the sun rising in the west?

Concorde in flight. *British Airways*